Stories Jesus Told

BY THE SAME AUTHOR

Absolutely Null and Utterly Void:
the Papal Condemnation of Anglican Orders 1896

Stewards of the Lord:
A Reappraisal of Anglican Orders

Man for Others:
Reflections on Christian Priesthood

Der priesterliche Dienst VI
Zur Frage der anglikanischen Weihen,.
(Quaestiones Disputatae 59)

Proclaiming the Good News:
Homilies for the "A" Cycle
Homilies for the "B" Cycle
Homilies for the "C" Cycle

Sea Psalms

Pontiffs: Popes Who Shaped History

STORIES JESUS TOLD

MODERN MEDITATIONS ON THE PARABLES

JOHN JAY HUGHES

LIGUORI, MISSOURI

Published by Liguori Publications
Liguori, Missouri
http://www.liguori.org

Library of Congress Cataloging-in-Publication Data

Hughes, John Jay.
Stories Jesus told : modern meditations on the parables / John Jay Hughes.
p. cm.
Includes bibliographical references.
ISBN 0-7648-0413-8
1. Jesus Christ—Parables—Meditations. I. Title.
BT375.2.H76 1999
226.8'06—dc21 98–54169

Printed in the United States of America
03 02 01 00 99 5 4 3 2

Contents

For the Sisters of Jesus Crucified
parables of faith
and
for Sebastian
a parable of love

Introduction

On April 3, 1954, I knelt before the Episcopalian Bishop of Newark, New Jersey, Benjamin M. Washburn—a prelate as godly as any I have known—to fulfill the dream I had cherished uninterruptedly from age twelve: to become a priest. In the formal exhortation which preceded the laying on of hands, the bishop told me in language that now seems stilted, yet which nourished me spiritually for more than three decades:

> And seeing that ye cannot by any other means compass the doing of so weighty a work, pertaining to the salvation of man, but with doctrine and exhortation taken out of the Holy Scriptures, and with a life agreeable to the same; consider how studious ye ought to be in reading and learning the Scriptures, and in framing the manners both of yourself, and of them that specially pertain unto you, according to the rule of the same Scriptures; and for the self-same cause, how ye ought to forsake and set aside, as much as ye may, all worldly cares and studies.

In the examination that followed, the bishop put to me this question, among others:

> Will you be diligent in Prayers, and in reading the Holy Scriptures, and in such studies as help to the knowledge of the same, laying aside the study of the world and the flesh?

> To which I replied, as required:

> I will endeavor to do so, the Lord being my helper.

Reflecting on the rite during my preordination retreat, I found this heavy emphasis on Scripture overdone and unrealistic. I accepted it as many Catholic ordinands accept the obligation of priestly celibacy—as part of a package deal. As the late Rudolph Bing, longtime general manager of New York's Metropolitan Opera, said about the nonnegotiable demand of a famous soprano that her husband conduct the orchestra for any opera in which she appeared: "If you want the meat, you have to take the bones with it."

More than four decades later I can see that this youthful view (like many others of which I was once confident but have since modified or abandoned) was mistaken. The years that have deepened my love for priesthood have also deepened my love of Scripture. The Church which required that I promise daily study and reading of Scripture as the indispensable support for priestly ministry was right to do so. Today I can affirm the promise I made long ago with an inner conviction I then lacked. Never have I regretted the step I took forty-four years ago: not for one single day.

My love for the priesthood is nourished by the celebration of the Eucharist. The desire to fulfill Jesus' command at the Last Supper to "Do this in my memory" planted the seed of a priestly vocation in boyhood. The daily fulfillment of that command remains for me today, next to my baptism, my pearl of great price.

Love for holy Scripture has been nourished by the ministry of preaching. For many years I preached weekly. For the past quarter century and more I have done so daily. Never am I happier than when the lectionary provides one of Jesus' parables as the gospel reading. Interest in the parables goes back as far as I can remember.

I am not a Scripture scholar. My academic training has been in church history. Like all those who write or preach about Scripture, scholars included, I stand on the shoulders of those who have gone before. My well-marked paperback edition of the classic work of Joachim Jeremias, *Die Gleichnisse Jesu*, acquired in 1968, has been used so much that the pages are falling out of the binding. Other books which have helped me will be found in the bibliography. Scriptural passages are quoted from the *New American Bible*, unless otherwise indicated.

The chapters that follow, though based on scholarship, are meditations. They are intended to be used as what monastic spirituality calls *lectio divina*—a term for which "spiritual reading" is inadequate but which, in the absence of a better translation, will have to serve. It is my hope that readers will find these pages useful supports for personal prayer.

The material has been adapted from retreat addresses given to the Sisters of Jesus Crucified in Newport, Rhode Island. Contemplatives in the Benedictine tradition, they are members of a congregation founded in France in the early 1930s for women with physical disabilities, which disqualify them from acceptance by other communities. Deeply prayerful, their courage and joyful faith are an inspiration to all who know them.

Readers who find any of my interpretations strained or unhelpful can take comfort in words written more than sixteen centuries ago by a far greater scriptural student and preacher than myself, the Syrian deacon Saint Ephraem:

> Lord, who can grasp all the wealth of just one of your words? What we understand is much less than what we leave behind, like thirsty people who drink from a fountain. For your word, Lord, has many shades of meaning just as those who study it have many different points of view. The Lord has colored his words with many hues so that each person who studies it can see in it what he loves. He has hidden many treasures in his word so that each of us is enriched as we meditate on it."[1]

John Jay Hughes
St. Louis, Missouri
Memorial of St. Augustine, 1998

CHAPTER 1

Teaching in Parables

ON ANOTHER OCCASION [Jesus] began to teach beside the lake. Such a huge crowd gathered around him that he went and sat in a boat on the water, while the crowd remained on the shore nearby. He began to instruct them at great length, by the use of parables, and in the course of his teaching said: "Listen carefully to this. A farmer went out sowing. Some of what he sowed landed on the footpath, where the birds came along and ate it. Some of the seed landed on rocky ground where it had little soil; it sprouted immediately because the soil had no depth. Then, when the sun rose and scorched it, it began to wither for lack of roots. Again, some landed among thorns, which grew up and choked it off, and there was no yield of grain. Some seed, finally, landed on good soil and yielded grain that sprang up to produce at a rate of thirty- and sixty- and a hundredfold" (Mark 4:3–8).

The previous chapters of Mark's Gospel report opposition to Jesus. "He commits blasphemy," the scribes complain when Jesus says to a paralyzed man, "Your sins are forgiven" (2:5, 7). Later in the same chapter the Pharisees ask Jesus' disciples why their Master eats "with tax collectors and offenders against the law"? (2:16). Two verses further on they want to know why Jesus' disciples do not fast like John's, and complain that they violate the law of Sabbath rest by pulling off heads of grain to eat (2:18, 24). When Jesus heals a man in the synagogue on the Sabbath, the Pharisees and Herodians plot "how they might destroy him" (3:6). A few verses further on his family say Jesus is "out of his mind" (3:21), and critics charge that his healings come from a pact with the Devil (3:22).

With the synagogue at Capernaum closed to him, Jesus adopts an unconventional mode of teaching: in the open air. The lakeside is a natural amphitheater. Sitting on the slope, everyone can see and hear Jesus in the boat a short distance from the shore. Since there were already critics watching his every move, it is not difficult to imagine pious people complaining that this method of teaching was undignified, even sensationalist. Jesus was always willing, however, to try new methods when the old proved unfruitful.

At a time of great national crisis, during the Great Depression of the 1930s, a new American president, Franklin Roosevelt, said that the nation's problems "demand bold, persistent experimentation. It is common sense to take a method and try it. If it fails, admit it frankly and try another. But above all, try something." The church could use more of this boldness. Too often, we cling to familiar ways of doing things out of fear that any innovation will be criticized or may not work. This excessive timidity has given rise to the jest about the Seven Last Words of the Church: "We never did it like that before." Never to have done it like that before proves one thing only: that we never did it like that before. It says nothing about how we should do it today, or tomorrow. Not all change is good. But to reject all change out of hand is a refusal to grow. No one has said it better than John Henry Newman: "To live is to change, and to be perfect is to have changed often."[1]

Jesus' willingness to adopt a new method of teaching when the traditional forum of the synagogue was closed to him is an example of his openness to change. Mark tells us: "He began to instruct them at great length, by the use of parables." "Parable" is derived from two Greek words: *para-bolé*. It means something which is placed alongside something else: in other words, a comparison. One definition of a parable might be: an earthly story with a heavenly meaning. Parables were Jesus' favorite form of teaching. Why? For three reasons:

I. Telling a story was a good way to capture people's attention. Jesus could not presume that his hearers would be attentive. Now that he was no longer speaking within the four walls of the synagogue, he had no captive audience. His hearers could walk away if they wanted to. He needed to seize their attention at the outset. He does so in this instance by saying to them: "Listen carefully to this" (4:3), and by immediately directing their attention to a farmer walking back and forth across his field in view of all: "A farmer went out sowing." Immediately the people are curious to know what Jesus will have to say about this man whom all can see. This is the first reason, then, why

Jesus taught in parables: to capture and hold people's attention.

II. Jesus also chose this method for greater intelligibility. He proceeds from something with which his hearers were familiar (in this case the farmer sowing seed in his field), to teach them about things less familiar. He uses a concrete image to convey an abstract idea. People think most easily in images. A teacher can talk at length about beauty without giving the pupils any clear idea of what beauty is. But show some examples—beautiful objects, scenes, paintings, sculpture, beautiful music—and these images will convey more than many words. We can talk a long time about human goodness; but concrete examples tell us more than long definitions. To give people an idea of what goodness is we talk not about virtues, but about people: Mother Teresa, Saint Francis, Jesus himself. In using concrete images Jesus was moving within the world of biblical thought, familiar to him from childhood. The Bible is always concrete, seldom abstract. When it talks about faith, it does so by describing people of faith. The eleventh chapter of Hebrews explains faith through sketches of faith-filled people. It speaks of Abraham, who "obeyed when he was called, and went forth...not knowing where he was going. By faith he sojourned in the promised land as in a foreign country, dwelling in tents [temporary dwellings, not solid houses]...for he was looking forward to the city with foundations, whose designer and maker is God" (Hebrews 11:8ff). The writer goes on to mention Moses, "who endured as seeing him who is invisible."[2]

The images Jesus used in his parables are so simple that they can be understood by children, yet so profound that scholars are still pondering them twenty centuries later. This is the second reason why Jesus liked to teach in parables: for greater intelligibility.

III. Finally, Jesus used parables as his favorite form of teaching because a story can stir consciences and get people consciously involved far better than moral exhortation. Jesus, who was intimately familiar with the scriptures of his own people, would have known this from the parable that the prophet Nathan told to King David, following the king's adultery with Bathsheba. She was the wife of Uriah, one of David's soldiers. While Uriah was off fighting for the king, David had an affair with Bathsheba. Upon learning that she was pregnant, David summoned her husband from the front. After asking for news of the war, the king plied Uriah with food and drink, hoping he would spend the night with his wife. Had David's stratagem succeeded, his adultery could have remained secret. Uriah would have assumed that the child born nine months later was his. Uriah refused to visit his wife, however, telling the king that he could not do so as long as his comrades were daily risking death in battle. Frustrated by the failure of his scheme, David then sent Uriah back into battle with secret orders to his commander which sealed Uriah's fate. Uriah was to be placed in harm's way, so that he would be killed in battle. To the original sin of adultery, a sin of weakness and passion, David added a far graver sin: cold, calculated murder. At this point God sends the prophet Nathan to King David with a parable:

> "Judge this case for me! In a certain town there were two men, one rich, the other poor. The rich

> man had flocks and herds in great numbers. But the poor man had nothing at all except one little ewe lamb that he had bought. He nourished her, and she grew up with him and his children. She shared the little food he had and drank from his cup and slept in his bosom. She was like a daughter to him. Now, the rich man received a visitor, but he would not take from his own flocks and herds to prepare a meal for the wayfarer who had come to him. Instead he took the poor man's ewe lamb and made a meal of it for his visitor." David grew very angry with that man and said to Nathan: "As the Lord lives, the man who has done this merits death! He shall restore the ewe lamb fourfold because he has done this and has had no pity" (2 Samuel 12:1–6).

With his reaction to the parable, David stands self-convicted. "You are the man!" Nathan tells him. Jesus, who was familiar with the passage, knew the impact of parables on the human conscience. He also knew that parables taught people *to think for themselves*. People who are *given* the answers to all their questions soon forget them. If they have to find the answer themselves, they are more likely to remember it. It is *theirs*.

Jesus' parables capture people's interest, then pose the challenging question: "How does this apply *to me*?"[3] A church that has feared innovation and change has also been afraid often to follow Jesus by challenging people to find their own answers. Jesus treated people as responsible adults. Too often the Church has treated them like children who must be given the answer to every question, even questions seldom asked. This encourages not virtue but moral laziness and immaturity.

Since the Second Vatican Council, Catholics are increasingly being challenged to find answers to problems and questions themselves. Church teaching is there to guide our decisions. It is up to us, however, using our God-given intelligence, to apply Church teaching to our own situation. For Catholics accustomed to having everything settled for them by authority, this is uncomfortable. The pain that such people have experienced in recent decades is the pain of growth. Such pain is necessary if we are, as Paul says, to "put childish ways aside" (1 Corinthians 13:11) and "be children no longer…[but] grow to the full maturity of Christ [our] head" (Ephesians 4:14f).

"Listen carefully to this. A farmer went out sowing." Jesus starts his teaching with a concrete example, most likely one within sight of his hearers. Jesus always taught like that. He moves from the familiar to the unfamiliar. He does not confuse people by starting with things that are strange and complicated. In this instance his starting point is intelligible even to children.

Jesus could teach like that because he knew that the world was *God's* world. He did not teach a religion of escape from an evil material world to some pure, spiritual realm. No. "God so *loved* the world that he gave his only Son…" (John 3:16). When Jesus looked out on the world, he saw everywhere the signs of its heavenly creator. Of course Jesus saw the evil in the world as well. How could he overlook this evil, when it meant opposition to him and his message, persecution, rejection, and crucifixion? When Jesus spoke of the suffering his followers would experience in the world, and then encouraged them with the assurance, "I have overcome the world" (John 16:33), he was speaking not of the good world of God's making. He was speaking of the evil world of human marring: the world organized apart from God, and against God.

Everywhere, however, Jesus saw in the world and in people reflections of his Father's love. He used the beauties of nature to teach God's loving providence: "Learn a lesson from the way the wild flowers grow. They do not work; they do not spin. Yet I assure you, not even Solomon in all his splendor was arrayed like one of these" (Matthew 6:28f). In the simplest gesture of human kindness, Jesus could see an act that merited a heavenly reward: "I promise you that whoever gives a cup of cold water to one of these lowly ones because he is a disciple will not want for his reward" (Matthew 10:42).

In taking his point of departure from the situation in which he spoke, Jesus shows that the essence of the parables is that they were spontaneous, unrehearsed, spoken on the spur of the moment. In this instance, Jesus, sitting in the boat and surveying the people arrayed before him on the lakeshore with a farmer scattering seed nearby, sees a point of contact with his hearers: something he can use to seize their attention, and to convey his teaching. Jesus' parables were not carefully polished and rehearsed, worked over in the quiet of the scholar's or poet's study. This makes them all the more remarkable.

Moreover, Jesus' parables were meant to be *heard,* not read. What is important is the overall impression, not the details. The parables are not allegories in which everything stands for something else. Rather they contain *one leading idea* that leaps out and strikes the mind at a first attentive hearing. To understand the parables it helps to ask: "What idea would flash into the mind of someone hearing this story for the first time?"

Once the parables were written down, it was natural that people should go back over them, finding significance even in the smallest detail. The parable of the sower is an excellent example. Originally a story about seeds, it has been transformed by the gospel writers into an allegory of different kinds of soil.[4] Those who heard the story for the first time had no time for reflection and analysis. It was enough for them to carry away one striking impression.

What might this impression be? It is the contrast between the waste of so much of the seed, and of the farmer's efforts—and the splendid harvest, despite all this waste. Consider Jesus' words again:

> Some of what he sowed landed on the footpath, where the birds came along and ate it. Some of the seed landed on rocky ground where it had little soil; it sprouted immediately because the soil had no depth. Then, when the sun rose and scorched it, it began to wither for lack of roots. Again, some landed among thorns, which grew up and choked it off, and there was no yield of grain. Some seed, finally, landed on good soil and yielded grain that sprang up to produce at a rate of thirty- and sixty- and a hundredfold.

The commentator in *The Jerome Biblical Commentary* explains: "A 20-to-1 ratio would have been considered an extraordinary harvest. Jesus' strikingly large figures are intended to underscore the prodigious quality of God's glorious kingdom still to come."[5]

The parable is Jesus' antidote to discouragement and despair. So much of our effort seems to be wasted. So much of the Church's work seems barren of result. The Christian community for which Mark wrote his gospel was discouraged, as we are often discouraged. Like Jesus himself when he first told the story, the Christians for whom Mark wrote had been banished from the synagogue that they loved, which was their religious home. They faced the same hostility as their Master. Jesus refused, however, to yield to discouragement. He remained confident—and told this story to give confidence to others.

It is for this that we read the story today. Are you discouraged? You have made so many good resolutions. Some you have kept. Many you have not. You seem to make no progress in prayer. When you come to confession, it is the same old list of sins. If that—or *any* of that—applies to you, then Jesus is speaking, through this parable, very personally to you.

"Have patience and courage," he is saying. "Do your work, be faithful to prayer, to your daily duties. God has sown the seed of his word in your life. The harvest is certain. When it comes it will be greater than you can possibly imagine. The harvest depends, in the final analysis, not on you, but on God. And God's seed is always fruitful, his promise always reliable."

Questions for Reflection

Am I too wedded to past ways of thinking, acting, praying?

Am I in a rut, "sot in my ways"?

Is there anything in my life that needs to change?

Am I afraid of change simply because it is new and I cannot see where it will lead me?

CHAPTER 2

JOY IN HEAVEN

"THE GRASS ALWAYS LOOKS GREENER on the other side of the fence." This familiar proverb expresses a universal human experience: the feeling we all have from time to time that our lives would be different, and better, "if only..." Different our lives would be. But better? Probably not. Entertaining this idea leads to "the Santa Claus illusion": the idea that some dramatic change will transform the dullness and mediocrity of our lives into joy, happiness, and fulfillment.

The Santa Claus illusion starts in childhood. A child who is doing poorly in elementary school nourishes the illusion that everything will be different when she gets into high school. When the difficulties continue there, she tells herself that the great transformation will come when she goes to college. Feeling her emotional needs unmet there, she imagines that everything will be better, "when I get rid of this creep I'm going with now and meet Mr. Right."

People frustrated by difficulties at work often think that everything will be wonderful if they change jobs or careers.

A young priest unhappy with an uncongenial pastor imagines that his troubles will vanish once he becomes a pastor himself. There are pastors who suppose that the difficulties of parish life would vanish if only the Church were discerning enough to make them bishops. And in religious communities it is not difficult to find people nourishing the illusion that community life will blossom and flourish with the advent of a new superior or the building of a new chapel or living quarters.

Looked at from the outside, it is easy to see that most of these hopes are unfounded illusions. This has given rise to the saying: "Be careful what you pray for. You might get it." The psalms, which are a remarkable treasure house of human experience and wisdom, refer to a striking example in the life of God's people. Disgusted at a steady diet of manna during their desert wanderings, the people tell Moses they want meat. Whereupon God sends them quails which, when eaten, make them sick (Numbers 11:33). "He gave them what they asked," the psalmist comments, "but sent a wasting disease against them" (Psalm 106:15). The Anglican Book of Common Prayer renders the verse more freely: "So he gave them their heart's desire, and sent leanness withal into their souls." This translation forcefully expresses what many have experienced, to their sorrow. The attainment of something long desired and prayed for did not bring the happiness and fulfillment they expected. Often it brought not fewer problems and frustrations, but more. The upper ranks of all large organizations, the church included, contain many sad examples of people disappointed in this way, some of them deeply embittered.

Yielding to the Santa Claus illusion—the idea that some dramatic change will transform everything and make life wonderful—is always mistaken. The people who entertain this illusion are not bad people. Most of them are good people. But they are looking for happiness in the wrong place: in a supposedly golden tomorrow, rather than in the humdrum, ordinary today. Nourishing ourselves with fantasies of a golden tomorrow means running the risk of dying without ever having lived to the full. The only time we have is today. It is here and now that we are to serve God and in so doing to find our happiness and fulfillment, not in some imagined wonderful tomorrow. When that tomorrow comes (if indeed it does), it, too, will be only another today.

Paul was teaching this lesson when he wrote to the Christian community at Corinth:

> As your fellow workers we beg you not to receive the grace of God in vain. For he says, "In an acceptable time I have heard you; on a day of salvation I have helped you." Now is the acceptable time! Now is the day of salvation! (2 Corinthians 6:1f).

Facing an operation for prostate cancer eight years ago, I was helped by the writings of the Yale surgeon, Dr. Bernie Siegel. He criticizes the training his own profession receives, in particular the idea shared by too many doctors: that death is the ultimate defeat. That is *wrong*, Siegel writes. Death is no defeat, for we must all die. The only true defeat is failing to live to the full *until* we die.

"I came," Jesus says, "that they might have life and have it to the full" (John 10:10). Is Jesus talking only about the future, about life after death? Don't you believe it! While ultimate fulfillment is reserved for a future life, the full life that Jesus is speaking about in that passage *begins here and now*.

Jesus' words about having come so that we might have life to the full are in the passage where he says he is the good shepherd. That is in John's Gospel. In Luke's Gospel Jesus tells a story about a shepherd's care for his sheep.

> The tax collectors and sinners were all gathering around to hear [Jesus], at which the Pharisees and the scribes murmured, "This man receives sinners and eats with them." Then he addressed this parable to them: "Who among you, if he has a hundred sheep and loses one of them, does not leave the ninety-nine in the wasteland and follow the lost one until he finds it? And when he finds it, he puts it on his shoulders in jubilation. Once arrived home, he invites friends and neighbors in and says to them, 'Rejoice with me because I have found my lost sheep.' I tell you, there will likewise be more joy in heaven over one repentant sinner than over ninety-nine righteous people who have no need to repent" (Luke 15:1–7).

This parable, and the two that follow (about the lost coin, and the longer one about the merciful father and the two lost sons), are Jesus' response to his critics' complaint: "This man receives sinners and eats with them." Jesus' association with such people was a scandal to his critics. To us, however, it is good news. We do not have to gain a passing grade in some moral examination before the Lord will receive, love, and bless us. He welcomes us just as we are: not because we are good enough, but because *he* is so good that he wants to share his love with us. Holy Communion, the most intimate fellowship we can have with the Lord in this life, is not a reward for good conduct. It is medicine for sick sinners. We could put up a sign in front of every altar the world over reading: "For sinners only, no others need apply."

It is important, however, that we approach the Lord's table *conscious* of our unworthiness. The Church helps us to do so by having us say before we approach,"Lord I am not worthy...." The Church requires further that if we are aware of deliberate sin in a grave matter we first seek reconciliation through the sacrament of penance. Failing to do so means refusal to recognize our unworthiness not only in general but in a specific area of our lives where, in a grave matter, we have deliberately turned our back on God (which is what mortal sin means). Paul was writing about such people when he said:

> Whoever eats the bread or drinks the cup of the Lord unworthily sins against the body and blood of the Lord. A man should examine himself first; only then should he eat of the bread and drink of the cup. He who eats and drinks without recognizing the body eats and drinks a judgment on himself. That is why many among you are sick and infirm, and why so many are dying (1 Corinthians 11:27–30).

The parable of the lost sheep begins with a question: "Who among you, if he has a hundred sheep and loses one of them, does not leave the ninety-nine in the wasteland and follow the lost one until he finds it?" The irony of

Jesus' question is lost on us. Those who heard the parable for the first time would have recognized it at once—and laughed. Tending sheep was not something that Jesus' critics would ever have stooped to. The shepherd had no time to keep all the provisions of the Jewish law. Such people, upset that Jesus received sinners and ate with them, looked down on shepherds. Challenging his critics with a question that forced them to look at things through the eyes of someone they scorned is an example of Jesus' use of humor.[1]

The question also assumes agreement: any responsible shepherd would act in the way suggested. In fact, acting thus—leaving the flock alone to search for the one lost sheep—would be the height of irresponsibility. That would risk turning a minor misfortune, the loss of one sheep, into a major disaster: the dispersal and possible loss of the entire flock.

What seems, by all standards of human and worldly prudence, wildly irresponsible is precisely the way God acts. God will go to *any* lengths to rescue the one lost sheep. God's love is not measured, prudent, reasonable. It is passionate, unconditional, unlimited: by human standards reckless. "*That* is why I receive sinners and eat with them," Jesus is telling his critics. "I am giving an example of my heavenly Father's all-consuming love."

The story's conclusion seems even more illogical: "There will be more joy in heaven over one repentant sinner than over ninety-nine righteous people who have no need to repent." Surely, we think, the ninety-nine should also be cause for joy—equal at least to the joy over the one repentant sinner. Indeed it is difficult to avoid the suspicion that the joy over the ninety-nine should be greater than that over the one. How can Jesus make such a rash statement?

To answer this question we must ask another. Who are the ninety-nine righteous people who have no need to repent? Do you know anyone like that? I do not. I know many people who *think* they have no need to repent. But they are wrong. Before God we all fall short. We all need to repent. People who fail to recognize this need are mistaken about their true spiritual condition. How can there be any joy in heaven over people who are so deluded?

So far we have been considering what the previous chapter called "the one leading idea" that strikes the mind of a person hearing the parable for the first time. It shows us that God's love is unbounded. God loves us so much that he is willing to act in ways that seem, by human standards, imprudent, even reckless.

The story has more to teach us, however. Just as the parable of the sower has been transformed, by reflection, from a story about seed into one about different kinds of soil, so reflection on the details of this story can take us farther, and deeper. So let's reflect.

The lost sheep is a picture of helplessness and dependence, for without the shepherd's care the animal's life expectancy is short. The sheep has wandered off without realizing it, in search of the greener grass which is always farther away. Once separated from the flock, the sheep, an animal of limited intelligence and easily frightened, is unable to find its way back. The sheep's bleating is a cry of helplessness. It cries for its companions. The shepherd knows, however, that the sheep is actually crying for *him*.

The lost sheep is a picture of the person who has strayed from God through mere thoughtlessness. We do not need bad intentions to lose our way. "The road to hell is paved with good intentions," as the old saying has it. Adolph Hitler deceived millions, in his own country and elsewhere, by proclaiming his good intentions. Upon assuming office as Germany's Chancellor in January 1933, he declared that he would make the two great churches in Germany, Catholic and Protestant, the cornerstone of his work of national renewal. He would clean up pornography, instill discipline in youth, put the unemployed to work, and restore a sense of national unity and purpose. It sounded wonderful. Small wonder so many were fooled.

Many people stray through carelessness, lack of self-restraint, thoughtless seeking after the greener grass which is always farther and farther away. The sheep bleating pitifully on the moor in the night is an image of the person who has wandered from the shepherd's care.

Jesus follows this parable with another, that of the lost coin:

> "What woman, if she has ten silver pieces and loses one, does not light a lamp and sweep the house in a diligent search until she has retrieved what she lost? And when she finds it, she calls in her friends and neighbors to say, 'Rejoice with me! I have found the silver piece I lost.' I tell you, there will be the same kind of joy before the angels of God over one repentant sinner" (Luke 15:8–10).

Jesus' choice of a woman as protagonist for this parable has a significance that is lost on us. Jesus lived in a man's world. As second-class citizens, the property of their fathers until marriage and thereafter of their husbands, women were ill suited to serve as examples of God's love. Despite occasional comparisons of God's love to that of a woman, therefore, the dominant image in the Jewish scriptures is of God as father. After shocking his pious critics in the previous parable by asking them to picture themselves as shepherds, he jolts them again by focusing on a woman. This disturbs the hearers' preconceptions and assures Jesus of their attention.[2]

The woman in Jesus' story is poor. The value of all ten coins is modest. And the fact that she must light an oil lamp to aid her search indicates that she lives in a small mud hut without windows. She sweeps the floor, itself of mud or possibly of flagstones, hoping to see the flash of the coin in the dim light, or to hear its clink in the darkness.

Was there a personal memory behind this detail? Did Jesus recall his mother searching anxiously for a small portion of the family's modest savings, and then inviting the whole village in to celebrate with her when the search was successful? We cannot know. Whether rooted in Jesus' personal experience or not, it is clear, however, that the expense of the celebration may well have exceeded the value of the coin first lost and then recovered.

This is Jesus' way of showing how utterly inadequate our ideas are for measuring the depth of God's love for us. For the woman to spend on a party more than the value of the coin she had lost and then recovered was, by any reasonable human standards, the height of folly. But not for God! "I tell you," Jesus says at the story's conclusion, "there will be the same kind of joy"—reckless, immoderate, foolish—"before the angels of God over one repentant sinner."

It is worthwhile reflecting farther on the lost coin, as we did on the lost sheep. It had *value* even after slipping from the hand of its owner. Once separated from the owner, however, the coin was of no *use*. Being inanimate, the coin had even less ability than the sheep to help itself. The coin got lost through falling from the woman's hand. Until then little force was necessary to keep it safe. The coin rested in the hand of its owner.

We are meant to be kept safe in God's hand. Apart from him, we have little power of our own to resist the downward pull of temptation, the inclination in each of us to follow not the good which, deep in our hearts, we really want but the evil which seems so attractive until we choose it. The theologians call this original sin. Paul described it in terms we all understand from personal experience:

> I cannot even understand my own actions. I do not do what I want to do but what I hate....This indicates that it is not I who do it but sin which resides in me. I know that no good dwells in me...; the desire to do right is there but not the power. What happens is that I do, not the good I will to do, but the evil I do not intend....What a wretched man I am! Who can free me from this body under the power of death? All praise to God, through Jesus Christ our Lord! (Romans 7:15–25).

Once the coin slipped from the owner's hand, it immediately fell. We were never meant to stand on our own feet, all alone against the attractions of evil. We were meant to be used by another, to be kept safe by a power greater than our own—a power coming from outside us, but active within us. Moreover, the coin, once lost, soon began to collect dust and tarnish. Though its real value does not diminish, someone finding it might mistake its value, thinking it base metal rather than silver or gold. God always sees our value beneath the grime even of our greatest betrayal and sin. To him we are infinitely precious. That is the story's first lesson—and also its last.

Questions for Reflection

How have I experienced God's loving care in my own life?

In what ways has God written straight on the crooked lines of my own unfaithfulness?

Am I really convinced of God's all-consuming love for me? Do I thank him enough for this love?

CHAPTER 3

The Merciful Father, the Two Lost Sons

JESUS SAID TO THEM: "A man had two sons. The younger of them said to his father, 'Father, give me the share of the estate that is coming to me.' So the father divided up the property. Some days later this younger son collected all his belongings and went off to a distant land, where he squandered his money on dissolute living. After he had spent everything, a great famine broke out in that country and he was in dire need. So he attached himself to one of the propertied class of the place, who sent him to his farm to take care of the pigs. He longed to fill his belly with the husks that were fodder for the pigs, but no one made a move to give him anything.

"Coming to his senses at last, he said: 'How many hired hands at my father's place have more than enough to eat, while here I am starving! I will break away and return to my father, and say to him, Father, I have sinned against God and against you; I no longer deserve to be called your son. Treat me

> like one of your hired hands.' With that he set off for his father's house.
>
> "While he was still a long way off, his father caught sight of him and was deeply moved. He ran out to meet him, threw his arms around his neck, and kissed him. The son said to him, 'Father, I have sinned against God and against you; I no longer deserve to be called your son.' The father said to his servants; 'Quick! bring out the finest robe and put it on him; put a ring on his finger and shoes on his feet. Take the fatted calf and kill it. Let us eat and celebrate because this son of mine was dead and has come back to life. He was lost and is found.' Then the celebration began" (Luke 15:11–24).

It is one of the world's great stories. The central figure is the father. The story's climactic scene is the father's welcome for his son. The picture of the younger son in his father's arms is Jesus' response to the complaint of his critics: "This man receives sinners and eats with them."

If we ask what the younger son had done to deserve such treatment from his father, the only possible answer is: Nothing. His return was motivated not by regret at having disappointed or hurt his father. Nor did he show any concern for the waste of his inheritance. He came home simply to put a roof over his head and food on his table. His carefully rehearsed speech was, at bottom, completely self-serving.

The younger son was, in reality, a confidence artist. Why did the father welcome him home with love? Not because the son deserved such a welcome, but because he *needed* it. Jesus welcomed tax collectors and sinners for the same reason: out of concern for their wasted, self-serving lives; to appeal, through love rather than through moral exhortation or condemnation, to the spark of goodness that was still in them as God's children.

The father's unmerited generosity to his selfish younger son is the strongest impression, surely, that a person hearing this story for the first time would carry away. Jesus was telling his self-righteous critics: "I welcome sinners and eat with them to show them my Father's love. The image of God imprinted on each human person at creation can never be completely obliterated. There is still a spark of the divine in even the most hardened sinner. By welcoming people you despise, who have done nothing to deserve my welcome, I am appealing to the element of goodness, however small, which is still in them as God's children."

Reflection on the story's details will uncover deeper levels of meaning not immediately apparent. So let's turn back to the beginning of the story, and reflect.

"Father, give me the share of the estate that is coming to me." The younger son's demand is peremptory. He wants what he wants when he wants it. He is tired of the dull routine at home. He wants to get out, to live it up, to do his own thing. That is the origin of every serious sin: the desire to do my own thing, in my own way, regardless of the cost. Sin arises from the mistaken idea that the only thing standing between me and happiness is inability to do my own thing. True happiness consists, on the contrary, in doing God's thing.

The younger brother's decision to leave home did not come overnight. It was the result of a long process of inner development of which we are told nothing, but which it is not difficult to imagine. Very likely there had been difficulties and rows already, attempts to run away, or at least threats to do so. Throwing over all the advantages of a secure and happy home can hardly have been the result of momentary dissatisfaction. More likely, years of complaining and resentment had nurtured a rebellious attitude that was present long before it was expressed openly. It was only a question of time before some trifle, a minor disagreement, precipitated the final breach and the younger son's decision to leave home. The psalms, that treasure house of wisdom, as we called them in the previous chapter, warn about the consequences of giving way to rebellion and resentment: "Calm your anger and forget your rage; do not fret, it only leads to evil" (36/37:8).

"So the father divided up the property." Why, we ask? Didn't the father know his son? Didn't he realize how ill equipped the boy was to use responsibly such a large sum as he was entrusting to him? The father knew that all too well. Wise, however, as many parents are not, he knew also that life's most effective school was also its hardest: the school of personal experience. He could have reasoned with his boy. He could have pointed out the dangers and pitfalls of what the young man was proposing. He knew that his son would not listen. Advice, however good, was wasted on him. The young man must find out for himself the difference between folly and wisdom. In this, too, the father in the story is like our heavenly father: he gave his son freedom to learn through personal experience. God does the same for us in giving us free will.

"Some days later this younger son collected all his belongings and went off to a distant land, where he squandered his money on dissolute living." With remarkable economy of words Jesus sketches a picture of sin and sin's consequences. The young man in the distant land is not only physically far away from his home. He has also distanced himself from the atmosphere of love that had surrounded him at home, and which he had mistaken for interference with freedom to do his own thing.

The new life is exciting at first. Soon, however, the young man encounters difficulties he had never anticipated. At home he had longed to be free. Now that he has his freedom, he finds it difficult to manage. He discovers forces within himself stronger than any he had imagined and impossible to control. The quest for excitement and thrills proves frustrating. Never quite satisfied, the young man is driven to seek ever greater thrills. Seeking freedom, he becomes in time a slave of passions more demanding than the dull routine he had chafed against at home. What a waste it all is. The young man supposed that once he had thrown off all restraints his life would be changed, and wonderful. Changed it was. Wonderful it was not.

We make a similar mistake when we deliberately seek spiritual experiences. These easily become a substitute for faith. The letter to the Hebrews defines faith as "confident assurance concerning what we hope for, and conviction about things we do not see" (11:1)—and, we might add, do not experience. As a general rule, spiritual experiences are given to three classes of people: those who are weak in faith and need encouragement; people who are undergoing severe trials; and those whom God is calling to specially onerous tasks. If we are trying to serve God he will give us all the spiritual experiences we need, though not necessarily all we want or think we need. Deliberately looking for such experiences, however, betrays lack of faith and produces inevitably the same kind of disappointment and frustration experienced by the younger son in this story.

"After he had spent everything, a great famine broke out in that country and he was in dire need. So he attached himself to one of the propertied class of the place, who sent him to his farm to take care of the pigs." To appreciate this detail of the story we need to recall that for Jesus and his hearers pigs were unclean animals whose flesh could not be eaten. For a Jew to have to tend pigs was the ultimate degradation. The young man has hit rock bottom.

"Coming to his senses at last, he said: 'How many hired hands at my father's place have more than enough to eat, while here I am starving!'" His concern is still for himself. To improve his lot he is willing to undergo a certain amount of embarrassment. He composes a speech in suitably obsequious terms. That will surely do it, he thinks. My father can hardly refuse to take me back as one of the servants. The old man was always a soft touch, he reflects.

"While he was still a long way off, his father caught sight of him and was deeply moved." How was it that the father saw his son a long way off? He was *looking* for him! How many times had he climbed the hill behind the house, when work was done, and looked down the road? And how many times had he turned back home with a heavy heart when no figure appeared over the distant horizon? This evening, however, someone does appear. Is it possible, the old man wonders? Could it be him? As the figure comes close, he recognizes him. It is really his son, come home again!

With a spring in his step that the father no longer knew he had, he runs down the road—something as unthinkable for the head of a family in Jesus' day as the spectacle of a bishop entering his cathedral on a skateboard would be in ours—to meet his boy and fold him in his arms. The father doesn't even allow the young man to finish his carefully rehearsed speech. Calling out to the servants in the house, he tells them to come quickly with fresh clothes and shoes. This detail, too, would have disturbed Jesus' hearers. In their world, day shoes were worn only by free people. Hired servants and slaves went barefoot. The father takes off his ring, the symbol of honor, and puts it on his son. The father, in other words, grants far more than his son's modest request. He transcends it. This is the heart of the story. The son in his father's arms is a picture of how much God loves us. The father's welcome continues as he orders a feast to celebrate his son's return.

A third character now appears:

> "Meanwhile the elder son was out on the land. As he neared the house on his way home, he heard the sound of music and dancing. He called one of the servants and asked him the reason for the dancing and the music. The servant answered, 'Your brother is home, and your father has killed the fatted calf because he has him back in good health.' The son grew angry at this and would not go in; but his father came out and began to plead with him.
>
> "He said to his father in reply: 'For years now I have slaved for you. I never disobeyed one of your orders, yet you never gave me so much as a kid goat to celebrate with my friends. Then, when this son of yours returns after having gone through your property with loose women, you kill the fatted calf for him.'
>
> "'My son,' replied the father, 'you are with me always, and everything I have is yours. But we had

to celebrate and rejoice! This brother of yours was dead, and has come back to life. He was lost, and is found'" (Luke 15:25–32).

The elder brother's anger at this unmerited welcome for his shiftless brother is fully understandable. The dialogue with his father that follows would have been as much of a jolt to Jesus' hearers, however, as the earlier picture of the father running. No self-respecting father in that patriarchal society would have left a celebration at which he was host to plead with his recalcitrant elder son. As head of the household, the father had the right to demand his son's presence, under pain of the severest sanctions if he refused.

Spurning his father's plea that he join the party, the elder son pours out a litany of bitter resentment, contrasting his own years of faithful service at home with his brother's scandalous rebellion. Though prevented by the father from doing so, the younger brother had resolved to ask for a place amongst his father's slaves. Now his elder brother's words claim that, in reality, that had been his own place all along: "For years now I have slaved for you." Could one really speak, however, of "slaving" for a father as loving and generous as this one? With his words, "everything I have is yours," the father shows how mistaken his firstborn is about their relationship.

We have heard nothing about loose women until now: the older brother is only too happy to supply this lurid detail. Most significant of all is his reference to "this son of yours"—as if to say: "your son, perhaps, but no brother of mine!" Is it not clear that the elder brother, too, is in a distant country, as far removed in his heart from his father's attitude of love as his younger brother had been physically distant?

The elder son had always resented his brother. When the latter left home, the elder brother's only regret was at his father's folly in entrusting this wastrel with money that he was clearly unfit to handle. Apart from that, his only thought was, *Good riddance*! The elder brother never noticed, and could not share, his father's grief at the younger son's absence. Now that he has reappeared, the elder brother is unable to share his father's joy and join in the celebration.

Before considering the story's conclusion it is worth pausing to reflect on the contrasting characters of these two brothers. The younger one is the type who is always yearning for the greener grass on the other side of the fence. Constantly seeking change and new experiences, he chafes at the all too familiar routine at home. When he looks at his elder brother, he sees not steadiness and perseverance but only hidebound conservatism, unwillingness to venture or dare. The elder brother's resistance to change of any kind may well be one of the factors that drove the younger one to leave home.

The elder brother is the type who values security before all else. There was no virtue in his refusal to leave home. He would never have contemplated such a move. That would have upset the placid course of his life. Better the petty frustrations I already know, he thinks, than the possibly much worse difficulties which might result from embarking on untrod paths. When he looked at his younger brother, the elder one saw only an irresponsible adventurer; a hopeless romantic who would come to no good end; someone willing to throw overboard the tried and true, with no notion of what might replace it.

Which of these two temperaments was better? The question can only be answered with another: "Better for what?" Each temperament has its advantages. Each has its drawbacks. What is crucial is something neither brother recognized: they *needed* each other. Without the irritant of the younger brother, the older one becomes a classical reactionary, distrusting anything new or different, clinging even to outmoded ways of doing things, simply because he is, on principle, against anything new, different, or unfamiliar. Alone, in isolation, he becomes intolerant, hardhearted, self-righteous. The proof of all this is his reaction to his younger brother's return.

Without the elder brother's steadiness, on the other hand, and his constant reminder of the value of tradition, the younger one becomes irresponsible. His desire for freedom and change becomes a purely selfish search for self-fulfillment without regard for the feelings or needs of others. The proof is his condition in the distant country: His quest for freedom has resulted in greater bondage than he ever experienced at home.

The two brothers have their counterparts in the Church today: and in every parish and religious community. The elder brother stands for all those who are threatened by change of any kind. They fail to grasp the truth of Newman's words, quoted in the first chapter: "To live is to change, and to be perfect is to have changed often." Believing themselves to be the embattled defenders of the faith, they spend their efforts too often defending not tradition in its fullness, but only what they themselves have experienced or what they find reported from the recent past. The critics who chided Jesus for "receiving sinners and eating with them" were of this type. Jesus portrayed the hardheartedness of the elder brother to show them what they had become.

The younger brother, on the other hand, stands for all those whose desire for change, renewal, and reform is irresponsible; who out of a mistaken concept of freedom ride roughshod over people with different temperaments or ideas; who delight in shocking those with whom they disagree; who do not realize that there can be good in tradition as well as in novelty.

Both brothers in the story end by losing joy—and losing touch, too, with their father: the younger one in the distant country, the elder while staying at home. This brings us to the story's conclusion. In fact, it has no conclusion. The story ends not with a reproach to the elder son but with the father's loving plea: "My son, you are with me always, and everything I have is yours. But we had to celebrate and rejoice! This brother of yours [a gentle reminder that he *is* still a brother] was dead, and has come back to life. He was lost, and is found."

How did the elder brother respond? Jesus does not tell us. He leaves the story without an ending, so that we can supply the conclusion ourselves.

Questions for Reflection

Have I heard the good news of our heavenly Father's freely given love?

Am I joining in its celebration?

CHAPTER 4

"Two Men Went Up to the Temple"

CHRISTIANS READING THE so-called Suffering Servant passages in the prophet Isaiah have always seen in them descriptions of Jesus Christ. Take the first of these passages:

> Here is my servant whom I uphold,
> my chosen one with whom I am pleased,
> Upon whom I have put my spirit;
> he shall bring forth justice to the nations,
> Not crying out, not shouting,
> not making his voice heard in the street.
> A bruised reed he shall not break,
> and a smoldering wick he shall not quench
> (42:1-3).

Jesus was like that. He dealt with people gently and sensitively. He took their difficulties seriously. Rather than giving them ready-made answers, he gave them the means to find their own answers. He received sinners and ate with them because he saw possibilities for good in people whom others, especially religious people, wrote off as hopelessly lost. Jesus is often called Teacher in the gospels. As teacher he made no mistake. He always spoke the right word to each person who came to him.

There was one class of people, however, with whom Jesus was not gentle but stern, even harsh: the Pharisees. The name means, literally, "the Separated Ones." They were probably given this designation by opponents because they insisted on strict separation from Gentiles, from people who were ritually unclean, from open sinners, and from those who did not keep the full Jewish law: the Torah, including oral interpretation of the law by the rabbis. Their stress on oral interpretation meant, however, that the Pharisees were flexible in their understanding of the law. They were the "liberals" in the Jewish community of their day. Scripture scholars believe that the negative portrayal of the Pharisees in the gospels reflects the tensions between synagogue and church at the time the gospels were written. They were actually better than the gospel portrayals lead us to believe.

> The gospel evaluation of the Pharisees, committed to writing in the last third of the first century, emerged in an apologetic context and is far too negative; it does not give the Pharisees sufficient credit for being the constructive force in Jewish spirituality that they really were.[1]

The twenty-third chapter of Matthew's Gospel, the most Jewish of all four gospels, is typical of this negative portrayal. It contains seven "woes" on the Pharisees, corresponding to seven of the beatitudes in the Sermon on the

Mount (Matthew 5:3–12). Jesus calls them "frauds" (often translated "hypocrites"), "sons of the prophets' murderers," "vipers' nest," and "brood of serpents"—a harsh indictment, indeed.

Contrast this with Jesus' treatment of open sinners. He refuses to condemn the woman caught in adultery, telling her simply: "From now on, avoid this sin" (John 8:11). He speaks similar words to the "woman known in the town to be a sinner" (Luke 7:37), who washed Jesus' feet with her tears and dried them with her hair. Criticized for his leniency by the Pharisee who was his host, Jesus declared: "Her many sins are forgiven—because of her great love. Little is forgiven the one whose love is small" (Luke 7:47).

A final example of this gentleness toward open sinners is Jesus' treatment of the Samaritan woman at the well in John's Gospel. When the woman says she has no husband, Jesus declares: "The fact is, you have had five, and the man you are living with now is not your husband. What you said is true" (John 4:18). Jesus allows the woman's disordered life to speak for itself. He does not condone, but neither does he condemn.

Jesus' frequent criticism of the Pharisees is the background for his parable of the Pharisee and the tax collector.

> He then spoke this parable addressed to those who believed in their own self-righteousness while holding everyone else in contempt: "Two men went up to the temple to pray; one was a Pharisee, the other a tax collector. The Pharisee with head unbowed prayed in this fashion: 'I give you thanks, O God, that I am not like the rest of men—grasping,

> crooked, adulterous—or even like this tax collector. I fast twice a week. I pay tithes on all I possess.' The other man, however, kept his distance, not even daring to raise his eyes to heaven. All he did was beat his breast and say: 'O God, be merciful to me, a sinner.' Believe me, this man went home from the temple justified but the other did not. For everyone who exalts himself shall be humbled while he who humbles himself shall be exalted" (Luke 18:9–14).

"Justified" in the story's conclusion means "put right with God." Our image of the Pharisees is so negative that we find nothing surprising in Jesus' evaluation of the two men. To his Jewish hearers, however, it was deeply disturbing, even shocking. Remember: the Pharisees were the specially religious people of their day. This is evident in the description of his piety which the Pharisee in this parable gives in his prayer. Fasting twice a week went far beyond the annual fast on the Day of Atonement stipulated in Leviticus 16:29. Paying tithes on everything one possessed also went far beyond what was required. Many things were exempt from the law of tithing.

We assume that the Pharisee was a hypocrite. Jesus' hearers knew better. They recognized that the man's account of himself was true. He really had done all these things. If a man like that was not right before God, the hearers would have asked, what hope was there for anyone?

Translated into modern terms, the Pharisee in Jesus' story was like a devout Catholic who goes daily to Mass and Communion, undertakes voluntary works of penance, and contributes a generous first portion of his income to church and charity. Even the Pharisee's prayer is good. It consists not of petitions but of thanksgiving. Recognizing that any virtue he has achieved has come to him only as a gift, he gives thanks to God for his blessings.

Jesus' hearers also recognized that the other man in the story was a real scoundrel. Their image of tax collectors was even more negative than our image of the Pharisees. Those who collected taxes in the Palestine of Jesus' day were not public servants, but corrupt entrepreneurs who contracted with the hated Roman occupiers of the country to supply a certain amount of revenue. They organized all kinds of shakedowns and protection rackets to maximize receipts, lining their own pockets in the process. The authorities cared little for these abuses as long as they enjoyed a sufficient cash flow. The tax collectors mentioned so often in the gospels were little better than racketeers. As such they were justly despised by all upright, respectable people. How shocked Jesus' hearers must have been, therefore, to hear him say that the corrupt tax collector went home from the Temple justified, while the pious Pharisee did not.

Why? Finding the answer will take us into the heart of the gospel. The simplest answer is simply this: The Pharisee does not receive God's free gift of justification because he sees no need of it. He has justified himself. He confuses goodness (which he possessed) with perfection (which he did not). This is a common failing in religious people. Instead of looking *up,* at the all-holy God, the Pharisee looks *around,* at others. Discerning, rightly, that others have not achieved his level of goodness, he looks *down* on his fellow worshiper in the Temple who, aware of how unworthy he is to stand in that sacred place, stands far off with bowed head, beating his breast in a gesture of humility as he pleads with God for mercy and forgiveness.

To compare ourselves with others is always a mistake. Such comparisons lead either to discouragement, when we find that others are better than we are; or to complacency, when we see that they are worse. Comparing ourselves with others is mistaken, too, because we do not know, and can never know, the difficulties against which others must contend. If I had been dealt the hand of the sister or brother who seems to have done so badly in life, can I be confident that I might not have done even worse?

To be truly close to God is to be keenly aware of one's unworthiness. The Pharisee in Jesus' parable failed this test. The young Isaiah, granted in an earlier Jerusalem Temple his vision of God "seated on a high and lofty throne, with the train of his garment filling the temple," was overwhelmed with a sense of his unworthiness: "Woe is me, I am doomed! For I am a man of unclean lips, living among a people of unclean lips; yet my eyes have seen the King, the LORD of hosts!" (Isaiah 6:1, 5). We encounter the same reaction in Peter at his miraculous catch of fish. Throwing himself at Jesus' knees, with the fish flopping all round him in the boat, Peter declared: "Leave me, Lord. I am a sinful man" (Luke 5:8). And Paul speaks for the saints of all ages when he calls himself "the least of the apostles; in fact, because I persecuted the church of God, I do not even deserve the name" (1 Corinthians 15:9).

We find similar protestations of unworthiness in all those whom we recognize to have been people of heroic virtue and holiness. How can we explain what looks to us like gross exaggeration? Is the humility of the saints a pose? Were they just pretending to be great sinners when in fact they were so much better than the rest of us? To answer these questions it helps to recall Jesus' words: "I am the light of the world" (John 8:12). If God is truly light, and his Son Jesus the prism through whose humanity we are able to look on a light too bright for any mortal to see and live,[2] then it is not difficult to understand that people who are close to this light see more of their sins than those who are far off.

A simple example from housework will make this clear. A table or other surface we have dusted can appear perfectly clean—until a ray of sunlight reveals an area we have overlooked. If the saints see their sins more clearly than the rest of us, this is because they are closer than we are to the One who calls himself "the light of the world" (John 9:5).

Despite his genuine goodness, the Pharisee is still distant from God's light. His conscience has fallen silent. He is one of the ninety-nine sheep in that other parable of the shepherd seeking the one sheep that has strayed. Comparing himself with the tax collector who comes to the Temple with him, the Pharisee sees no need of repentance. This is why his prayer is not heard. Because of his spiritual blindness there is no joy over him in heaven—and there can be no joy. It is the Pharisee's complacency which explains Jesus' condemnation at the story's conclusion. Despite his piety and good works, the Pharisee is still not right with God. He goes home from the Temple unjustified.

The tax collector, on the other hand, has done evil and is objectively bad in a way that the Pharisee is not. There is hope for him, however, because he is dissatisfied with his condition. He has lost even the sinner's last protection: self-respect. He knows that he is shunned by all decent people, and for good reason. In his despair he turns to the only one who will not shun him—to God.

Humanly speaking, the tax collector's situation is hopeless. According to Jewish law, he had not only to repent of his sin but to restore to those he had defrauded all he had stolen, plus 20 percent. He has no list of victims and amounts. And besides, most if not all of the money is already spent. In this hopeless situation he turns to the only one in whom he still dares to hope—to God.

In doing so he uses the opening words of Psalm 51: "God, be merciful to me." According to Jewish tradition, this psalm was King David's prayer of repentance after he had committed adultery with Bathsheba and killed Bathsheba's husband. Verse 19 of the psalm says: "A heart contrite and humbled, O God, you will not spurn." Jesus gives us this parable to assure us that those words are *true*. That is how good God is. He will never spurn or shun anyone, no matter how steeped in sin, who comes to him asking for mercy and forgiveness. God accepts even the most hopeless, despairing sinner. He rejects only those who are fully satisfied with themselves. God, Jesus is telling us through this story, is the God of the despairing; of those whose situation is, humanly speaking, hopeless. He is the God of those who seem to make no progress in virtue or prayer, who cannot overcome their bad habits and addictions. There is no limit to his goodness toward those whose hearts are broken.

If the parable is a warning, as Luke tells us in his introduction, "to those who believe in their own self-righteousness while holding everyone else in contempt," it is even more an encouragement to people who see no reason to hope. It is the Lord's way of telling us: "Do not be discouraged because you are not the person you would like to be. Your sins, failures, compromises give you a claim on God—on me as God's Son and representative—provided that you frankly admit your sins. Never fear the dark forces within you that have led you to sin so often. Fear one thing only: the Pharisee's inner peace and self-satisfaction. It is the peace of death—of a dead conscience."

Questions for Reflection

Do I often compare myself with others? Finding encouragement when I see others worse than I am, or discouragement when I see others who are better?

Do I often bring my failings and sins to God, asking for his mercy and forgiveness? Or do I try to run away from and hide the things in my life that cause me embarrassment, humiliation, and shame?

CHAPTER 5

"Which Did What the Father Wanted?"

"WHAT DO YOU THINK of this case? There was a man who had two sons. He approached the elder and said, 'Son, go out and work in the vineyard today.' The son replied, 'I am on my way, sir'; but he never went. Then the man came to his second son and said the same thing. This son said in reply, 'No, I will not'; but afterward he regretted it and went. Which of the two did what the father wanted? They said, 'The second.' Jesus said to them, 'Let me make it clear that tax collectors and prostitutes are entering the kingdom of God before you. When John came preaching a way of holiness, you put no faith in him; but the tax collectors and the prostitutes did believe in him. Yet even when you saw that, you did not repent and believe in him'" (Matthew 21:28–32).

On the day after Christmas, 1958 Angelo Roncalli, who had become Pope John XXIII not quite two months before, visited Rome's central prison—called in typical Roman fashion *Regina Coeli*, "Queen of Heaven." There is nothing heavenly about a prison. In this one there was pandemonium on the day of the pope's visit. "I was hemmed in on all sides," the pope wrote in his diary the next day, "authorities, photographers, prisoners, guards—but the Lord was close."[1]

A murderer managed to ask the pope: "Can there be forgiveness for me?" The Holy Father responded by enfolding the man in his arms. No words were necessary. The embrace said it all.

"You can't come to me," Pope John told the prisoners when the hubbub which greeted him quieted down. "So I have come to you." He went on to tell them that he had some personal experience of jails: his brother had once been arrested for poaching. In the account of the visit that appeared in the Vatican newspaper *Osservatore Romano* the next day, this remark was censored. The editor feared that readers would be scandalized to learn that a pope's brother had been in trouble with the law. The man's red pencil was wielded often in the next four years, crossing out similar papal indiscretions from the copy that crossed his desk.

To John the visit to the prison was simply an exercise of one of the works of mercy, commanded by Jesus in the parable of the sheep and goats: "I was...in prison and you came to visit me" (Matthew 25:36). His diary expressed surprise at the media reaction: "The press, Italian and international, continue to exalt my gesture in visiting the prison yesterday. And for me it was such a simple and natural thing."

Pope John's experience with the religious establishment, represented in this instance by the editor of the Vatican newspaper, was not unlike that of Jesus Christ. "Tax collectors and prostitutes are entering the kingdom of God before you," Jesus said to the religious leaders of his people at the end of this short parable about the man with two sons. He was addressing "the chief priests and elders of the people." They had challenged Jesus with the question: "On what authority are you doing these things? Who has given you this power?" Jesus responded with a counterquestion: Was John's baptism human or divine? Jesus' critics recognized at once the threat this question posed to them. If they acknowledged that the Baptist had possessed divine authority, Jesus would ask why they had not accepted him. If, on the other hand, they said that John's authority was merely human, they would discredit themselves with the people, who regarded John as a prophet. To Jesus' question they replied, therefore, "We do not know." Jesus responded, "Then neither will I tell you on what authority I do these things" (Matthew 21:23–27).

Matthew places this exchange toward the close of Jesus' public ministry. Jesus' association with people of bad moral character (represented here by "tax collectors and prostitutes") had scandalized his pious critics from the start, as we have already seen. His acceptance of such people did not mean approval of their sinful lives, any more than Pope John's embrace of the murderer implied approval of violent crime. By welcoming notorious sinners Jesus was appealing to the spark of goodness that was still in them as God's children. He knew that kindness and love can break through the hardened human heart far more effectively than moral denunciation.

The parable of the two sons was Jesus' way of bringing home the contrast between the religious leaders, who rejected him, and the outcasts of society, who heard him gladly. To Jesus' hearers, living in a patriarchal society, the father in the story was a figure of unquestioned authority. His sons owed him obedience not merely because they lived in his house. Obedience was also a sacred duty enjoined by the fourth commandment: "Honor your father and your mother."

The first son's obedience is respectful and prompt. Addressing his father as "Sir" (Matthew uses the Greek word *kyrios*, "Lord"), he says he is on his way. "But he never went," Jesus tells us. With no further word, the father then turns to his second son. There is nothing respectful about this one's response. "No, I will not," he says brusquely—an in-your-face refusal of his duty, which would have deeply shocked Jesus' hearers. As in the case of the first son, however, there was a gap between what this second son said and what he did. "But afterward he regretted it and went." Matthew's Greek text is briefer, consisting of four words only: "Later repenting he went."

Jesus immediately confronts his critics with a question. "Which of the two did what the father wanted?" They cannot evade this time, as they had done when questioned about John the Baptist. Jesus' critics give the only possible answer: "The second." They are convicted out of their own mouths, like David waxing indignant at the prophet Nathan's story of the rich man taking the one lamb of his poor neighbor to entertain a guest. "The man who has done this merits death," David had said on that occasion. "You are the man!" Nathan told him at once, reminding the king that he had done worse. He had stolen another man's wife and had her husband killed (2 Samuel 12:5–7). Jesus' words to his critics are no less direct than Nathan's to King David:

> I assure you [literally "truly I tell you," a formula of special solemnity] tax collectors and prostitutes are entering the kingdom of God before you. When John came preaching a way of holiness, you put no faith in him; but the tax collectors and prostitutes did believe in him. Yet even when you saw that, you did not repent and believe in him.

The first son in the story, who told his father he was on the way to work and then failed to go, is like Jesus' upright critics. Proud to be members of God's chosen people, they were confident that faithful performance of their religious duties gave them a claim on God which he was bound in justice to honor. They had forgotten that we never have a claim on God. God has a claim on *us*, and it is an absolute claim. "When you have done all you have been commanded to do," Jesus says on another occasion (and which of us has?), "say, 'We are useless servants. We have done no more than our duty'" (Luke 17:10).

The story's second son, who told his father there was no way he was going to work for him any longer, and later regretted his insolence and went to work after all, is like the depraved outcasts who heard Jesus gladly. Their lives proclaimed rebellion against God. But the welcome they gave Jesus showed there was still goodness in them. Jesus appeals to this goodness by his compassionate love. Perhaps, like the second son, they will yet feel regret and turn from the darkness of their wasted lives to the sunshine of God's forgiveness and love. This hope is the basis for Jesus' stern warning to his hardhearted and self-righteous critics: "Tax collectors and prostitutes are entering the kingdom of God before you."

For us the story contains both warning and encouragement. Faithful performance of our religious duties—the Precepts of the Church and obedience to God's commandments—is in itself no guarantee of salvation. Such obedience is profitable only if it brings us closer to others and makes us more loving people—and if it brings us closer to God. And the closer we come to God, the more clearly we shall recognize our remaining sinfulness and unworthiness of all the love he showers on us. The story's warning is the same one Jesus uttered in the Sermon on the Mount: "None of those who cry out, 'Lord, Lord,' will enter the kingdom of God but only the one who does the will of my Father in heaven" (Matthew 7:21).

To whom does Jesus direct this warning? Who are those who cry, "Lord, Lord"? Certainly not the declared enemies of Jesus Christ. No, *we* are the people Jesus is addressing here, and in the parable of the two sons as well. Day by day, Sunday by Sunday, and month by month, we utter the Lord's name: in petitions, intercession, thanksgiving, praise, and penitence. That is right and good. The parable warns us, however, that if our piety does not bear fruit in our lives, we are still far from God. The warning is not for outsiders, for others. It is for us, the declared followers of Jesus Christ.

If the story's first son is a warning to us, however, the second son is an encouragement. As followers of Jesus Christ we have been taught that readiness to respond to God's' call is a virtue, slowness or refusal a sin. Complaining is to be avoided, and with it the rebellious attitude which both produces and nurtures complaints. Few of us, however, avoid these things completely. Often we have been slow to respond to God's call, manifested to us through the inner voice of conscience, through the needs of a sister or brother whom we encounter along life's way, or in the legitimate commands or requests of those in authority. There are times when we have refused such calls altogether.

All that is, in the last analysis, of little account, Jesus is telling us—or rather of no account at all. What counts is not what we say, feel, or intend. The only thing that counts is what we *do*. Negative feelings, resentment of God's demands or of the demands of others, are not important if, despite such feelings, we are trying to do what we know is right. Indeed, being generous with God and others when this is difficult, in spite of the sullen resentment within, is of *greater* value than obeying God's call in times of spiritual fervor and zeal.

God sees the difficulties with which we must contend. When we stumble and fall, and think we can rise no more because we have been down so often before, we need to ask God to do *for* us what we can no longer do ourselves. When we approach God in that way we *do* have a claim on him: the claim of a sinner seeking God's mercy. Then we are like the tax collector praying in the Temple in the other parable: "O God, be merciful to me, a sinner." That is one prayer that is always heard, and always granted. We have Jesus' word for it: "Believe me, this man went home from the temple justified...." (Luke 18:14).

Questions for Reflection

Do I sometimes think my good works give me a claim on God which he is bound to honor?

What is there in my life (if anything) which *does* give me a claim on God?

How do I handle resentment of the demands made on me: by God, the Church, other people?

CHAPTER 6

"I Canceled Your Entire Debt"

Abbot Jerome Kodell, of New Subiaco Abbey in western Arkansas, describes an ugly scene at the funeral of a widow. Two of her adult children refused to attend because their siblings were also present. What a terrible picture of family bitterness and unhappiness. The cause? Inability to forgive past wrongs and injuries, even at the grave of the common mother.

"Lord, when my brother wrongs me," Peter asked Jesus one day, "how often must I forgive him? Seven times?"

In the thought world of the New Testament the number seven was symbolic. Peter was suggesting a number which, though not taken literally, still assumed that the duty of forgiveness had limits somewhere.

"No," Jesus replied, "not seven times; I say, seventy times seven times" (Matthew 18:21–22). Multiplying Peter's suggestion by itself and then again by ten, Jesus was saying that for his followers the duty of forgiveness was unlimited. There was never a time when the Christian disciple could say, "I have forgiven enough. Now is the time not for mercy but for justice." Peter had asked about the quantity of forgiveness. Jesus did not really answer Peter's question. Instead he told a story about the *quality* of forgiveness, and the reason for it.

> "That is why the reign of God may be said to be like a king who decided to settle accounts with his officials. When he began his auditing, one was brought in who owed him a huge amount. As he had no way of paying it, his master ordered him to be sold, along with his wife, his children, and all his property, in payment of the debt. At that the official prostrated himself in homage and said, 'My lord be patient with me and I will pay you back in full.' Moved with pity, the master let the official go and wrote off the debt. But when that same official went out he met a fellow servant who owed him a mere fraction of what he himself owed. He seized him and throttled him. 'Pay back what you owe,' he demanded. His fellow servant dropped to his knees and began to plead with him, 'Just give me time and I will pay you back in full.' But he would hear none of it. Instead, he had him put in jail until he paid back what he owed. When his fellow servants saw what had happened they were badly shaken, and went to their master to report the whole incident. His master sent for him and said, 'You worthless wretch! I canceled your entire debt when you pleaded with me. Should you not have dealt mercifully with your fellow servant, as I dealt with you?' Then in anger the master handed him over to the torturers until he paid back all that he owed.

> My heavenly Father will treat you in exactly the same way unless each of you forgives his brother from his heart" (Matthew 18:23–35).

The story's opening is ominous. A king, for Jesus' hearers, was not a constitutional monarch with limited powers, but a man with power of life and death over his subjects. The people with whom he intends to settle accounts are important officials responsible for collecting the king's taxes. "One was brought in," the story says. The use of the passive suggests that official is hauled before the ruler by the royal guards.

The amount of the man's debt would have caused Jesus' hearers to gasp in disbelief. The "vast amount" in our translation conceals the exact amount named by Matthew: "ten thousand talents." A talent was the largest sum of money then in use—something like a million dollars today. The king they knew best, Herod the Great, is estimated to have had a total annual income of only nine hundred talents. To have incurred a debt more than ten times that already huge amount meant that the official had been embezzling on an enormous scale. To find a modern equivalent we might imagine that the District Commissioner of Internal Revenue for New England has managed to divert for his own use all the income tax receipts of his six states for an entire year.

A debt of that magnitude is unpayable. As the story says, "He had no way of paying it." The king's command, that not only the official but his wife and children as well, should be sold into slavery, shows that this was a tyrannical Gentile monarch. According to Jewish law only a robber unable to restore what he had stolen could be enslaved. Other family members were immune from such punishment.

Up to this point in the story, the sympathy of Jesus'

hearers would have been with the corrupt official. Though his embezzlement of such a huge sum was dishonest, the king's cruelty was worse. The man's plea, "My lord, be patient with me, and I will pay you back in full"—reinforced by his body language: prostrating himself before the king in homage—bears no relation to reality and is merely an expression of the official's desperation. Once a sum of money so vast was gone, a lifetime would have been insufficient to repay it.

Now comes a surprise: "Moved with pity, the master let the official go and wrote off the debt." A king who was prepared to enslave an entire family for the debt of one member is not the kind of man from whom Jesus' hearers would have expected mercy, let alone mercy on this scale. So it is nonetheless. The story will have further surprises still.

No sooner delivered from his desperate plight, the official, formerly passive ("brought in"), becomes active: "he went out." Matthew's Greek text ("going out, that servant found one of his fellow servants") permits us to imagine the first official looking for the colleague who owed him money. Again Matthew states the amount. The "mere fraction" of our translation is, in the original, "a hundred denarii." A denarius was a day's wage—the amount promised by the vineyard owner in another parable to those hired early in the day (cf. Matthew 20:2). The contrast with the debt owed by the first official, and now forgiven, and that owed the latter by his colleague is immense.

The second official's reaction to the demand that he pay his debt mirrors that of the first. Body language (kneeling) and plea ("Just give me time and I will pay you back in full") are identical. The sole difference is that the second official's debt could easily be paid, given reasonable time. How shocking for those hearing the story for the first time to learn of the first official's harsh response. Seizing his colleague by the throat and throttling him, he insists that the man be imprisoned until the debt is paid. The first official has completely forfeited the sympathy he enjoyed at the story's outset.

In the story's conclusion the colleagues of the two debtors do what Jesus' hearers wish they might do in the same situation. They report the injustice to the king. Summoning the first official again, the king reminds him of the unmerited mercy he has received and, in an act of grim irony, grants the man what, in his original desperation, he had requested: time. Now, however, the time will be spent not in repayment but in prison, under torture.

It is a story of contrasts. The contrast between the king's mercy and his servant's cruelty is obvious. Less clear is the contrast between mercy and justice. The story moves back and forth between the two. The king's original summons and the command that the corrupt official, with his whole family, be sold into slavery are an insistence on justice at any price. The official reacts to his sentence on the same level. Instead of appealing for mercy, he pleads, however unrealistically, that given time justice will be done: "Be patient with me, and I will pay you back in full."

The hearers of the story are surprised when the king, portrayed up to this point as cruel, abandons his insistence on justice and shows mercy, granting his corrupt official not what he had asked (time to pay the debt) but *more* than he had asked (forgiveness of the debt). Justice required that, in return, this official grant his colleague's plea for time to pay the relatively small amount which he owed.

The corrupt official's refusal of this plea violates *both* justice and mercy—the more so since the plea, in this case, was reasonable and realistic. This double failure brings on him swift and terrible retribution.

Behind the king in the story stands God. The corrupt official's hopeless plight parallels our own. From birth we owe God everything. He has given us the gift of life, using our parents as his instruments, and the unique set of gifts and talents with which each of us is endowed. Only a life of perfect obedience to God could discharge this debt. By *disobedience*, however, we have incurred further debts. Like the first official in the story, our situation is hopeless. Our debt to God is unpayable. Out of pity for our plight, God sent his Son to pay on our behalf a debt we could never discharge ourselves. God has done for us, in short, what the king did for his corrupt official. As Paul writes, "He pardoned all our sins. He canceled the bond that stood against us with all its claims, snatching it up and nailing it to the cross" (Colossians 2:13–14).

This free gift of forgiveness is not a reward for anything we do. It is simply an expression of God's overflowing love for us as his children—sinful yet still his own, created in his image. This forgiveness is given to us, like all God's gifts, under one strict condition: that what we have freely received, we freely *share* with others. The story's lesson is simple: If we are not forgiving toward others, as God is *already* forgiving toward us, we risk discovering one day that the forgiveness God has extended to us has been *canceled*. Jesus is telling us, in short, that our treatment of others, here and now—and especially of those who have wronged us—is already determining where, how, and with whom we shall spend eternity.

God's forgiveness of our unpayable debt begins in baptism. For the forgiveness of debts incurred thereafter—through serious postbaptismal sin—there is another sacrament: penance or reconciliation. Confession, as we know it today, is the result of centuries-long development: No other sacrament has undergone such sweeping changes as this one. Reflecting on this sacrament can help us deepen the lesson of the parable we have been considering.

For many Catholics sacramental confession is a routine if somewhat burdensome obligation. For others it is an unpleasant duty which we tend to put off because it is painful, but which, finally performed, makes us feel better afterward. In reality the sacrament of penance is so much more. It is a *personal encounter with One who loves us beyond our imagining*—an encounter every bit as intimate as the reception of holy Communion. The one to whom we confess our sins is Jesus himself. The priest is only his representative. His role in forgiveness resembles that of the letter carrier who brings our mail. Forgiveness comes not from the priest, but from God. His forgiveness is free. But it is not cheap. It cost the lifeblood of God's son, Jesus Christ.

People often complain of the impersonal quality of modern life. Many Catholic parishes support this feeling. Too large to develop the closeness and warmth of Protestant congregations, most of them far smaller, Catholic congregations are often gatherings of more or less anonymous individuals rather than welcoming communities. No wonder that many feel they are "just a number." In the sacrament of penance, however, we are *not* just a number. Through his priests, the Lord receives us one by one.

One of the things emphasized in priests' training is that the person in the confessional *right now* is more important than others who are waiting. This does not mean allowing someone with merely routine sins to run on indefinitely. It does mean, however, that in cases of real need or gravity, the priest must take all the time necessary, regardless of how many are still waiting.

That is the ideal, admittedly. Confessors are as susceptible to impatience as parents are with their children—a sin often confessed, incidentally, especially by those with young children. A young priest in India remarked after hearing over eight hundred confessions before Christmas: "You can't show impatience, even when you feel impatient." That is beautiful. No less beautiful is something a newly ordained priest wrote to a friend still in seminary: "I go into the confessional now, and experience God in a completely new way."

Speaking for myself—yet also, I know, for many of my brother priests—I can say that despite the tedium and boredom of so much confessional practice, there are sometimes tears in my eyes as I listen to the struggles of fellow sinners to reconcile with God and others, or to pick themselves up and go on after the most humiliating falls. What is it that brings them to disclose even secret sins in the hearing of a fellow sinner? There is only one possible answer. They are drawn, like steel filings to a magnet, by the One whose love will never let us go. His forgiveness is instantaneous and total. "Though your sins be like scarlet, / they may become as white as snow; / Though they be crimson red, / they may become white as wool" (Isaiah 1:18). Human forgiveness is always partial: A memory of the injury remains, a skeleton in the closet. Not so with God: "I will forgive their evildoing and remember their sin no more" (Jeremiah 31:34).

Which of us has not been discouraged at falling back again into sins we have confessed so many times before? "It's the same old list, Father" a penitent will say in the confessional. To this common complaint there are two responses. First, committing the same sins time and again is at least better than sinning in ever new ways. And second, it is important to understand what the sacrament of penance does for us, and what it does not do. Absolution takes away sin's *guilt*. It does not remove sin's *consequences*. God immediately takes away guilt from a student who confesses the sin of laziness (to take an example which is especially easy to understand). But the consequences of the student's sin remain: ignorance of the neglected material, and bad study habits. Such consequences must be repaired over time—which is why theologians call them sin's "temporal punishment." We do not go away different people. We take away the same weaknesses of character that we brought with us. With forgiveness, however, God gives us his help to repair these weaknesses. Doing so requires patience and perseverance. The struggle against sin continues until life's end. God does not call us to be successful in this struggle. He calls us to be faithful. "The man who holds out to the end will be saved" (Matthew 24:13, *Jerusalem Bible*).

We leave the confessional with a priceless gift: forgiveness. If we act like the first official in Jesus' story, we shall lose this gift. To keep it, we must share it with others. We can put it even more strongly. We *cannot* keep the gift of God's forgiveness—*unless we give it away!*

Questions for Reflection

Do I ever reflect on how much I owe God, and how much he has forgiven me?

Am I forgiving with others? Or do I tend to hold grudges?

Have I ever refused to forgive, even after an apology?

CHAPTER 7

"I Want My House to Be Full"

PROFESSIONAL JOURNALISTS tell novices at their trade, "When you have a good story, run it every once in a while." This dictum explains why newspapers are still printing accounts of such long-ago events as the assassination of President Lincoln, the crash of the German zeppelin *Hindenburg*, the abdication of Britain's King Edward VIII (the later Duke of Windsor) to marry "the woman I love"—and the sinking of the *Titanic*. The last story furnished material for a blockbuster film, a vehicle for Hollywood's special effects, and for an improbable but maudlin love story which has littered movie theaters the world over with tear-drenched paper handkerchiefs.

Like all preachers, Jesus told his stories more than once, often giving them a different spin in the retelling. His story of the great supper is a case in point. In Luke's Gospel the host is a social climber jilted by his friends who tries to get back at them by staging a party with guests whom none of those originally invited would have cared to meet socially. In Matthew the story is more dramatic—and violent as well. The host is a king who holds a wedding banquet for his son. When the invited guests kill the royal servants who bring the invitation, the king takes revenge by executing the murderers and burning their city. Matthew's version also has a sequel: When the host finds one of his substitute guests improperly attired, he has him thrown out into outer darkness. We shall consider Luke's version of the story.

> He went on to address a parable to the guests, noticing how they were trying to get the places of honor at the table: "When you are invited by someone to a wedding party, do not sit in the place of honor in case some greater dignitary has been invited. Then the host might come and say to you, 'Make room for this man,' and you would have to proceed shamefacedly to the lowest place. What you should do when you have been invited is go and sit in the lowest place, so that when your host approaches you he will say, 'My friend, come up higher.' This will win you the esteem of your fellow guests. For everyone who exalts himself shall be humbled and he who humbles himself shall be exalted."
>
> He said to the one who had invited him: "Whenever you give a lunch or dinner, do not invite your friends or brothers or relatives or wealthy neighbors. They might invite you in return and thus repay you. No, when you have a reception, invite beggars and the crippled, the lame and the blind. You should be pleased that they cannot repay you, for you will be repaid in the resurrection of the just."
>
> At these words one in the party said to him, "Happy is he who eats bread in the kingdom of God." Jesus responded: "A man was giving a large

> dinner and he invited many. At dinner time he sent his servant to say to those invited, 'Come along, everything is ready now.' But they began to excuse themselves, one and all. The first one said to the servant, 'I have bought some land and must go out and inspect it. Please excuse me.' Another said, 'I have bought five yoke of oxen and I am going out to test them. Please excuse me.' A third said, 'I am newly married and so I cannot come.' The servant returning reported all this to his master. The master of the house grew angry at the account. He said to his servant, 'Go out quickly into the streets and alleys of the town and bring in the poor and the crippled, the blind and the lame.' The servant reported, after some time, 'Your orders have been carried out, my lord, and there is still room.' The master then said to the servant, 'Go out into the highways and along the hedgerows and force them to come in. I want my house to be full, but I tell you that not one of those invited shall taste a morsel of my dinner'" (Luke 14:7–24).

Jesus told the story, according to Luke, as a guest at table himself. Noticing his fellow guests engaging, upon arrival, in a scramble for places of honor at the table, Jesus pretends to be doing them a favor by giving them shrewd advice. Staking a claim to a prominent seat is too risky, Jesus counsels. Your host might ask you to give way for someone more important. That would be embarrassing. Your best move is to sit down modestly in the lowest place. You won't risk being displaced there. And with any luck at all your host will invite you to move up to a better place. Your fellow guests, impressed first with your modesty, will be impressed a second time at the host's demonstration of your importance.

In reality, Jesus was giving this seemingly shrewd advice "tongue in cheek." Can we imagine Jesus caring *where* he sat at table? If there is one thing Jesus certainly was not, it was a snob. By *seeming* to take seriously the scramble for social success, Jesus was actually holding it up to ridicule. He was showing up snobbery for the empty and shabby affair it always is.

The advice had a deeper significance, however. Jesus was really talking about our relationship with God. His opening words give the clue: "When you are invited to a wedding party...." In the Jewish scriptures God's relationship with his people is often portrayed in terms of marriage. "I will espouse you to me forever... / in love and in mercy... / in fidelity," God said through the prophet Hosea (2:21–22). Though Israel proved unfaithful to its marriage bond with the Lord, God remained faithful:

> The Lord calls you back,
> like a wife forsaken and grieved in spirit,
> A wife married in youth and then cast off,
> says your God.
> For a brief moment I abandoned you,
> but with great tenderness I will take you back
> (Isaiah 54:6–7; cf. 62:4f, where the metaphor appears again).

Ezekiel's long chapter 16 compares Israel's unfaithfulness to God to the behavior of an unfaithful wife who has become a harlot. Despite this unfaithfulness, however, God remains faithful.

> Yet I will remember the covenant I made with you when you were a girl...I will re-establish my covenant with you...that you may be utterly silenced for shame when I pardon you for all you have done, says the Lord GOD (Ezekiel 16:60–63).

Isaiah portrays the messianic age, when God will send his anointed servant to visit his people, in terms of a feast:

> On this mountain the LORD of hosts
> will provide for all peoples
> A feast of rich food and choice wines...
> ...he will destroy
> the veil that veils all peoples....
> The Lord GOD will wipe away the tears from all faces (Isaiah 25:6–8).

The Church gives us this passage on the twenty-eighth Sunday in Ordinary Time, Year A, when the gospel reading is Matthew's version of the great supper story which we are considering. The prophets used the image of a divine banquet to say that the sins of God's people would not always estrange them from the all-holy God. A time would come when God would take away sins, so that people could enjoy fellowship with God.

Jesus' story about a banquet was a way, therefore, of saying that he had been sent by God to fulfill what the prophets had promised. The banquet was ready. The Pharisees were confident that the best seats at the banquet were reserved for them. Hadn't they earned them? They observed the law meticulously. They even went far beyond its requirements. Jesus' seemingly shrewd advice about how to achieve social success was a rebuke to those who assumed that they had first-class tickets to the banquet. Jesus was warning them that they were in for a surprise—and that it would be unpleasant.

In what follows, Jesus expands this warning. When you are giving a dinner yourself, he says, don't invite relatives and friends who can return your hospitality, and important people whose presence at your table feeds your self-esteem. Invite instead people who cannot repay you, guests whose presence in your house will not enhance your reputation in society.

Jesus supported this advice with his own example—and was criticized for it. "This man welcomes sinners and eats with them," his critics complain at the beginning of the following chapter in Luke's Gospel (15:2). Jesus acted as he did to show that this is how God treats all his children. He invites *everyone* to the feast, not just those whom we consider deserving. My heavenly Father, Jesus says in the Sermon on the Mount, makes his sun rise "on the bad and the good, he rains on the just and the unjust" (Matthew 5:45)—images from nature readily understood by Jesus' hearers who lived in an arid land, dependent on sunshine and rain for sustenance and livelihood.

The people who were scandalized by the company Jesus kept were consistent at least. They refused to associate with Jesus' disreputable companions. His story about the man giving a large dinner is addressed to these critics. Some commentators suggest that the host in the parable was a tax collector himself. He has made a lot of money. His party was an attempt to break into society by inviting the leading citizens of the town and providing lavish entertainment. His guests have all told him, in the offhand way that people do, that they'd be happy to come to his house. "Ask me any time," they had all said.

When the invitations arrive, however, it turns out that these acceptances were insincere. The excuses offered are flimsy. The guest who pleads that he must inspect the land he has just bought would presumably have done this before the purchase. The same is true of the man who says he must test his newly purchased oxen. His acquisition shows that he is a prosperous farmer. Today's equivalent of five yoke of oxen would be an expensive combine for cutting and threshing wheat—equipment worth over one hundred thousand dollars. The man who is newly married seems to have the best reason for declining. He doesn't want to leave his wife. Dinner parties in Jesus' day were for men only. Moreover, Jewish law gave special consideration to male newlyweds, exempting them from military service (cf. Deuteronomy 24:5).

Jesus' hearers would have smiled as they heard of the frustration of the host's plans. He thought he was going to make a big splash. One after another, all his guests have stood him up. The man's growing anger enhances the humor of the situation. He resolves to repay the insults of his intended guests with an insult of his own. He will give a party for people whom those originally invited would hold in contempt. That will show them!

The description of these substitute guests would have caused further smiles. They are the very people Jesus has just told his social climbing fellow guests that *they* should invite, rather than those who could return the invitation, or people so wealthy or important that their mere presence would be a reward. The substitute guests are "the poor, the crippled, the blind, and the lame." When there are still empty places after the arrival of this tacky company, the host's final revenge on those who have snubbed him is to invite the homeless. "Go out into the highway and along the hedgerows," he instructs his servant, "and force them to come in. I want my house to be full." In a final expression of anger the host announces: "Not one of those invited shall taste a morsel of my dinner."

The parable, like many others, contains a warning—but also good news. The warning is the exclusion of those first invited. They represent Jesus' critics: people confident that the best seats at the banquet were reserved for them. Too busy to claim their places just now, they assume that there will be other opportunities, other invitations. Too late, they discover they are wrong. This was their final chance, and they have missed it. Now they are excluded forever.

The parable's good news is contained in the description of the substitute guests. Luke's Gospel is specially concerned with the poor and marginalized. "Blest are you poor," Jesus declares in the Sermon on the Plain (6:20). When John the Baptist sends disciples from prison to ask whether Jesus, so different from the Messiah he expected, is really "He who is to come" (7:19), Jesus responds by citing his ministry to the poor and weak:

> Go and report to John what you have seen and heard. The blind recover their sight, cripples walk, lepers are cured, the deaf hear, dead men are raised to life, and the poor have the good news preached to them (7:19, 22).

These are the people Jesus recommends to his socially ambitious fellow guests as fitting recipients of their hospitality. And they are also the people who enjoy the host's hospitality in the parable. Reading the story today, we can see Luke's description of the substitute guests as a portrait of his own Christian community: "not many of you are wise...not many influential; and surely not many well-born," to cite Paul's words from his first Letter to the Corinthians (1:26).

For us, the parable's good news is its assurance that God welcomes not just the fit and strong, people whose good moral character makes them role models and leaders. The Lord who was reproached in his earthly life for welcoming sinners and eating with them continues to do the same to-day. To claim a place at his table we need to show him not our successes but our failures; not our strength but our weakness; not health but sickness. For (to quote Paul again)

> God chose those whom the world considers absurd to shame the wise; he singled out the weak of this world to shame the strong. He chose the world's lowborn and despised, those who count for nothing, to reduce to nothing those who were something; so that mankind can do no boasting before God (1 Corinthians 1:27–29).

Questions for Reflection

Do I worry more about what others think of me than of how I stand before God?

What promptings of conscience, or opportunities for service, am I postponing to deal with later, "when I've got more time"?

Am I offended by some of the people I see coming to Mass and Communion on Sunday?

CHAPTER 8

Law or Love?

On one occasion a lawyer stood up to pose him this problem: "Teacher, what must I do to inherit everlasting life?" Jesus answered him: "What is written in the law? How do you read it?" He replied:

> "You shall love the Lord your God
> with all your heart,
> with all your soul,
> with all your strength,
> and with all your mind;
> and your neighbor as yourself."

Jesus said, "You have answered correctly. Do this and you shall live." But because he wished to justify himself he said to Jesus, "And who is my neighbor?" Jesus replied: "There was a man going down from Jerusalem to Jericho who fell prey to robbers. They stripped him, beat him, and then went off leav-

> ing him half-dead. A priest happened to be going down the same road; he saw him but continued on. Likewise there was a Levite who came the same way; he saw him and went on. But a Samaritan who was journeying along came to him and was moved to pity at the sight. He approached him and dressed his wounds, pouring in oil and wine. He then hoisted him on his own beast and brought him to an inn, where he cared for him. The next day he took out two silver pieces and gave them to the innkeeper with the request: 'Look after him and if there is any further expense I will repay you on my way back.'
>
> "Which of these three, in your opinion, was neighbor to the man who fell in with robbers?" The answer came, "The one who treated him with compassion." Jesus said to him, "Then go and do the same" (Luke 10:25–37).

The parable is so well known that its title, "The Good Samaritan," has entered into everyday speech. Even people unfamiliar with the New Testament know that "a good Samaritan" is someone who helps a person in need. The man whose question, "What must I do to inherit everlasting life?" sets the stage for the parable is "a lawyer." He was not what we understand by that term, however. This lawyer studied *God's* law: the Ten Commandments plus the centuries of learned reflection on the law by the rabbis, called in Hebrew *midrash*. The man's question reflects the Jewish understanding of God's law. Observance of the commandments meant *life*, Moses told the people when he gave them the Ten Commandments. Disobedience led to death.

> I have set before you life and death....Choose life, then, that you and your descendants may live, by loving the LORD, your God, heeding his voice, and holding fast to him (Deuteronomy 30:19f).

God's commandments are not a fence to hem people in. They are ten words of wisdom, signposts to human fulfillment and happiness. This was Jesus' understanding of the law. As a boy in the synagogue school at Nazareth he would have learned, very likely by heart, what Moses' had said about the commandments:

> "Observe them carefully, for thus will you give evidence of your wisdom and intelligence to the nations, who will hear of all these statutes and say, 'This great nation is a truly wise and intelligent people.' For...what great nation has statutes and decrees that are as just as this whole law which I am setting before you today?" (Deuteronomy 4:6–8).

Asked about the conditions for everlasting life, Jesus poses a counterquestion: "What is written in the law? How do you read it?" As a good teacher, Jesus knew that people remember best the answers they have found themselves. Answers given by the teacher cost the questioner nothing and are easily forgotten. By directing the lawyer's attention to God's law, in effect Jesus was telling him, "You already know the answer."

The lawyer's response shows that he is familiar with rabbinical discussion about which of the 248 commandments enumerated in midrash commentary on the original ten was "most important." He combines two scriptural texts: the command to love God completely in Deuteronomy 6:5 and the command to "love your neighbor as yourself" from Leviticus 19:18. Jesus' reply affirms both this answer and the view that observance of God's law leads to life: "You have answered correctly. Do this and you shall live."

The lawyer says, however, that he still has a difficulty. It is not a moral difficulty—*how* to love God and neighbor. That is no problem for him. His difficulty is intellectual: How far does his obligation extend? "And who is my neighbor?" With his unique ability to read hearts and minds, Jesus perceives the man's real difficulty at once. By assuming that he has all the ability to love that is required and needs only to know the limits to which he must extend his love, the man has disclosed that in reality his love is seriously deficient.

Jesus might have told the man that his question, "And who is my neighbor?" showed how little love he really had. He might have scolded the man for his hardheartedness. Either response would have put the man on the defensive and encouraged not the change of heart he needed, but self-justification. Another approach would have been to answer the man's question by telling him bluntly: "You must love everybody." Even if the lawyer had been able to accept an injunction so sweeping, however, he would still have made no progress in learning love's meaning. Extending his obligation would bring no change of heart. Jesus recognizes that what the man really needs is not instruction but conversion. His real difficulty lies not in his head (as the man supposes), but in his heart.

To deal with this difficulty Jesus ignores the question, "And who is my neighbor?" With great tact, and without allowing the man to feel rebuked, Jesus tells a story. The central figure and hero turns out to be an outsider: some-one despised both by the questioner and by Jesus' hearers, a man who knew little of the Jewish law or midrash, yet who fulfilled their spirit better than those who were experts in both.

The seventeen-mile road from Jerusalem to Jericho leads, even today, through trackless sand dunes with no sign of human habitation, except for the occasional Bedouin tent. On foot it was a five-hour journey at least. In Jesus' day, robberies and muggings were frequent along this lonely way. In the prevailing daytime heat a severely wounded man's chances of survival were slim without first aid. The victim in this story has been beaten and stripped of his clothes. He has lost much blood and is in shock. He lies unconscious, his condition critical. Jesus himself calls the man "half dead."

The first two travelers to come by, first a Jewish priest and later a Levite, are returning to Jericho, a town with a large population of clergy, after their eight-day tour of duty at the Temple in Jerusalem. Our translation says that the priest saw the wounded man "but continued on." The Levite, too, "saw him and went on." Luke uses the same verb in both cases. It means literally "passed by opposite." This suggests that they crossed to the other side of the road, unwilling even to approach the unconscious victim.

We need not assume that they were indifferent to the man's fate. They might have feared that the muggers were still lurking nearby, waiting to strike again. In that case it would be best not to linger. Another motive for not stopping, especially if the man was dead, was unwillingness to incur ritual impurity through touching a corpse. Jewish law forbade such contact for priests, except for the case of near relatives (cf. Leviticus 21:1–4). Violations of this law required lengthy purification rites.

In Jesus' day, as in ours, stories often had three characters. We have all heard jokes about a Protestant minister, a Catholic priest, and a rabbi—or about a Franciscan, a Dominican, and a Jesuit. Following the appearance of two clergy, therefore, the hearers would expect that the next passerby will be a Jewish layman. If he had stopped to help the man, the story would have an anticlerical thrust. This would have appealed to the audience, since priests and Levites were objects of resentment in Jesus' day. As so often, however, Jesus confounds his hearers' expectation.

The modern equivalent of the priest and Levite in the story would be a priest and a deacon. When the next passerby turns out to be a Samaritan, it had the effect on Jesus' hearers that the trio, priest-deacon-Chinaman, might have on us. Even that comparison hardly captures the shock Jesus' hearers would have experienced on learning the identity of the third passerby. The hostility between Jews and Samaritans was notorious. Modern parallels would be the hatred between Serbs and Croats, or between Israeli settlers and Palestinian militants. The gospels give evidence of this hostility in several places. When Jesus' critics want to insult him, they call him "a Samaritan, and possessed [of a devil] besides" (John 8:48). The enmity was mutual. Shortly before the passage we are considering, Samaritan villagers refuse to give Jesus lodging, "because he was on his way to Jerusalem" (Luke 9:53).

Devout Jews had a special aversion for Samaritans because, though ethnically related to God's people, they did not recognize the Jewish prophets and did not observe God's law. The actions of this Samaritan show, however, that he is living the law's spirit far better than Jesus' questioner with all his knowledge of the law's letter. Like the priest and Levite, the Samaritan "sees" the man. Unlike them, however, he is "moved to pity." The verb Luke uses is a strong one. He has used it three chapters before to describe Jesus' reaction to the widow at Naim, preparing to bury her only son: "seeing her, the Lord *had compassion* on her" (Luke 7:13, literal translation). Luke uses the same verb in the parable of the Prodigal Son to describe the father's reaction to his son's return: "his father caught sight of him and *was deeply moved*" (Luke 15:20, italics added).

The Samaritan shows his compassion by applying the medicinal elements available to him: oil for its soothing properties, wine as a disinfectant. Taking the victim to the nearby inn, a refuge for travelers unable to complete their journey in one day, he ministers further to the man, remaining with him overnight. Jesus makes this clear by saying that the man gave the innkeeper two silver pieces "the next day." Commentators have calculated that this would pay for the man's care for twenty-four days. His injuries are obviously grave if he must remain so long. Innkeepers in Jesus' day had a reputation like that of taxi drivers in certain big cities today. Without this generous payment, and the Samaritan's promise that he would return to take care of any further expenses—but also, surely, to check on the man's recovery and make sure he had been treated properly—the victim would have been at the innkeeper's mercy.

As the story ends, Jesus has still not answered the lawyer's question, "And who is my neighbor?" Instead he has shown how a true neighbor behaves. He remains tactful with his questioner, however. He might have asked:

"Which of these three most resembles yourself?" Such a question would have put the lawyer on the defensive, blocking the change of heart he needed. Continuing the approach he has used from the start, therefore, Jesus puts a different question. Rather than confronting the lawyer with a lesson difficult for him to accept, Jesus invites the man to draw his own conclusion

"Which of these three, in your opinion, was neighbor to the man who fell in with robbers?"

The answer is clear: "the Samaritan." We see just how difficult it was for the man to state the obvious, with its uncomfortable implications, from the fact that he cannot even utter the name of the despised outsider. He resorts to a circumlocution: "the one who treated him with compassion."

Only at this point, when the man has himself stated what no one hearing the story could fail to grasp, does Jesus confront him directly: "Then go and do the same." At last the man has his answer—though even now only by implication. His neighbor, the one who has a claim on him—on his time, his trouble, his purse—is anyone at all who is in need. The man had asked about the limits of neighborly obligation. The parable says in effect: "There are no limits."

That is breathtaking. It *would* be breathtaking, that is, if the story's sharp cutting edge had not been dulled for us, like so much of Scripture, by familiarity. How, we ask, can Jesus make such a radical demand? For one reason alone: because this is the way he, Jesus Christ, treats *us*. From the time of Augustine, preachers and commentators have seen behind the figure of the Samaritan in this story the figure of Jesus himself. *Jesus* is the despised outsider, hated and rejected by those who ought to have known, recognized, and welcomed him.

Jesus is the one who finds us lying bruised, battered, mortally wounded along life's way. Without the help that he alone can supply, our situation is hopeless. For no merits of our own, but simply because of his infinite compassion, Jesus comes to our aid. Heedless of the cost to himself, he binds up our wounds, pouring upon us the healing oil of his forgiveness in the sacraments of baptism and penance, the exhilarating wine of his love in his holy word and in the Eucharist. He entrusts us to the care of his Church, promising to come again and again as often as may be necessary, to tend to our every need.

Because of this total generosity toward us in our need, a readiness to help which caused Jesus to lay down his life for us, he is able to say to us: "See how much I have done for you—look what I am doing for you even now! Then go and do the same for others."

The lawyer's question, "And who is my neighbor?" showed his real failing. He was unable to get beyond the law's details. To be cured, he needed to encounter the Lawgiver. His name is Jesus Christ.

Questions for Reflection

From what dangers, great and small, have I been saved in my life? If the help has come through others, who sent them to me?

When I was saved through circumstances, who was it who arranged things so that I am here today?

How can I share with others the care and compassion I have experienced myself?

CHAPTER 9

"Surprised by Joy"

In the middle years of the twentieth century there was no more articulate spokesman for Christian faith writing in English than C. S. Lewis. A professor of English literature, first at Oxford then at Cambridge, he died in 1963. His books still enjoy large sales today. In his only autobiographical work Lewis tells how he moved from the dry and formal Protestantism of his childhood in Northern Ireland to abandonment of all religious belief in his teens. When he was past thirty, Lewis became a believer again: first in God, then in Jesus Christ as God's Son. Lewis was a faithful member of the Anglican Church for the rest of his life. He called the book in which he related his spiritual journey *Surprised by Joy* (1955). Lewis chose this arresting title to describe his discovery of something which had been there all along, without his realizing it. The title was also a tribute to the wife whom Lewis, a confirmed bachelor most of his life, married in 1956 at age fifty-eight: Joy Davidman Gresham. The film *Shadowlands* tells the story of their marriage.

Two of Jesus' briefest parables are about people surprised by joy. The first is poor, the second rich.

> "The reign of God is like buried treasure which a man found in a field. He hid it again, and rejoicing at his find went and sold all he had and bought that field. Or again, the kingdom of heaven is like a merchant's search for fine pearls. When he found one really valuable pearl, he went back and put up for sale all that he had and bought it" (Matthew 13:44–46).

The first man is a day laborer, plowing his employer's field. As he walks back and forth across the familiar ground, the plow catches on something which he takes, at first, to be a rock. Investigation shows that it is actually a pottery jar, filled with valuable coins. In a world without banks or safe-deposit boxes, guarding valuables against robbers was difficult. When Jesus spoke, in the Sermon on the Mount, about thieves who "break in and steal" earthly treasure, the word translated "break in" means literally "dig through" (Matthew 6:19). Jesus' hearers understood him at once. A thief could easily tap the mud wall of a Palestinian house to locate a hollow spot, and then dig through to steal the valuables concealed within. For most people, therefore, the best means of safekeeping was to bury things in the ground.

People who had buried valuables might die unexpectedly—in war, or as victims of violent crime—before telling anyone where the treasure was located. Finding buried treasure was thus the equivalent, in antiquity, of winning the lottery today: something dreamed of by thousands, though experienced by few.

Who has buried *this* treasure and when, the laborer in Jesus' parable cannot know. He knows at once, however, that the find can change his life, giving him the first financial security he has ever known. He realizes also, however, that he has a problem. Both Roman and Jewish law stipulated that buried treasure belonged to the owner of the land where it was found. Carrying the jar home would be too dangerous. Should his employer learn of the find, he would surely claim it for himself. Carefully, therefore, the man reburies the jar, somewhat deeper this time, noting the location, and goes on with his work. Once he gets home, he scrapes together his meager savings and makes his employer an offer to buy the field. He is careful to seem casual about it, so as not to arouse suspicion. When the offer is accepted, he is overjoyed. The purchase has cost everything he has. The treasure which is now his, however, is worth far more.

The pearl merchant is at the opposite end of the social-economic scale. A wealthy man, he has amassed a fortune at his trade. Unlike the day laborer, he is *looking* for treasure: Finding it at a reasonable price, and selling it at a higher price, is his livelihood. He may have started as a youngster, collecting stones that caught his fancy. That is far behind him now. He smiles as he recalls the worthless trinkets that interested him long ago. For years now he has limited his business to pearls. Retrieved by divers from the Red Sea, pearls were, next to gold, the greatest treasure of the ancient world. The author of the first Letter to Timothy mentions pearls immediately after gold as examples of ostentatious adornment unsuitable for women in the Christian community (cf. 1 Timothy 2:9). Pearls are also mentioned several times in the book of Revelation, each time as examples of luxury and splendor (cf. Revelation 17:4; 18:12, 16; 21:18–21).

Walking through the bazaar one day, the merchant sees a pearl so large and flawless that it takes his breath away. Buying it will require liquidating his entire stock. No matter. He is confident he can sell it eventually at a still higher price. When you have found perfection, he reflects, no price is too high.

That is not so far-fetched as it sounds. Some of today's most successful art dealers have established their reputations by buying high and selling higher still. When wealthy collectors told the British art dealer, Lord Duveen, that they could buy a Rembrandt or a Renoir from a competitor at a lower price, he would tell them condescendingly, "Yes, but it wouldn't be a Duveen." In the world of the superrich it was an argument that enjoyed remarkable success.

Common to both men in these two little parables is the feeling of joy. Though both had to sell all they had, neither thought for a moment of the sacrifice he was making. Each thought only of the joy of his new possession. They knew it would change their lives forever. Common also to both parables is the introductory phrase, "The kingdom of heaven is like...." The comparison is not so much with the treasure gained as with the willingness of each man to sacrifice all to gain the treasure—and to do so not regretfully, but with joy.

When we think only of the price we must pay to be loyal to Jesus Christ, we make the practice of our faith grim and forbidding. In these two linked parables, as beautiful as they are brief, Jesus is emphasizing not the cost, but the infinitely greater reward. Down through the ages the greatest Christians have been people like the men in these two parables: happy to sacrifice all for Jesus Christ, because of the joy of life with him, and for him.

In the ancient world there is Augustine, born in North Africa in 354 to a Christian mother and a pagan father. Endowed with a brilliant mind, Augustine grew up unbaptized, sensing the attraction of Christianity throughout his twenties, but thinking the price of Christian discipleship too high. Finally baptized at thirty-three, he wrote years later in his *Confessions*, addressing himself to God:

> How sweet did it become to me all at once to be without those trifles! What I previously feared to lose, it was now a joy to be without. For you cast them away from me, you true and highest sweetness. You cast them out and instead entered in yourself, sweeter than all pleasure (*Confessions* ix,1).

An example of a man "surprised by joy" in our century is the German Jesuit Alfred Delp, who gave his life for Jesus Christ on February 2, 1945, under the tyranny of Adolf Hitler. In a farewell letter, written with manacled hands in his prison cell under sentence of death but full of joy and peace, Father Delp spoke of *his* great discovery and changed perspective:

> I know now that I have been as stupid and foolish as a child. How much strength and depth I have sacrificed in my life! How much fruitfulness I might have had in my work, how much blessing I might have given to others! Only the person who believes, who trusts, who loves, sees truly what human life is really all about. Only he can truly see God.[1]

The English convert G. K. Chesterton writes in his own inimitable style of joy as the distinguishing mark of the Christian, and the inner secret of Jesus Christ.

> Joy, which was the small publicity of the pagan, is the gigantic secret of the Christian...The tremendous figure which fills the Gospels towers in this respect, as in every other, above all the thinkers who ever thought themselves tall. His pathos was natural, almost casual. The Stoics, ancient and modern, were proud of concealing their tears. He never concealed his tears; he showed them plainly on his open face at any daily sight, such as the far sight of his native city. Yet he concealed something. Solemn supermen and imperial diplomatists are proud of restraining their anger. He never restrained his anger. He flung furniture down the front steps of the Temple...Yet he restrained something. I say it with reverence; there was in that shattering personality a thread that must be called shyness. There was something that he hid from all men when he went up a mountain to pray. There was something that he covered constantly by abrupt silence or impetuous isolation. There was some one thing that was too great for God to show us when he walked upon our earth; and I have sometimes fancied that it was his mirth.[2]

Television allowed millions the world over to witness the outpouring of public grief at the tragic death of the British Princess Diana in September 1997. Grief fueled the protest of the London crowds that there was no flag at half mast over Buckingham Palace. Courtiers explained that the only flag permitted there was the Royal Standard, which is flown only when the sovereign is in residence. Since the Queen was in Scotland, the flagpole remained bare. Within days, however, tradition yielded to sentiment. For the first time ever, the Union Jack flew over Buckingham Palace, and at half mast.

The followers of Jesus Christ have a royal standard, emblazoned with the single word: "Joy." It flies above the Christian heart, to show that the King is resident within.

Questions for Reflection

Would those who know me best say I am a joyful person? If not, why not?

At times when I cannot *feel* joy, do I crawl into my shell and wallow in self-pity?

Do I continue trying to reach out to others, even when this is difficult because of the burdens I am carrying?

CHAPTER 10

"I Knew You Were a Hard Man"

Jesus' story about the plowman finding buried treasure reflected a practice as common in Jesus' day as the purchase of life insurance or contributions to a pension plan are in ours. Save for those few wealthy enough to afford strong rooms and guards, the best way for the ordinary person in the ancient world to safeguard a treasure was to bury it in the ground. A person entrusted with the custody of valuables belonging to someone else fulfilled his duty by burying what he had been given. Jesus' hearers would have been shocked, therefore, by his story about a man who was punished for what anyone in that day would have called correct behavior.

Jesus introduces the story by saying it is about a man going on a journey:

> "He called in his servants and handed his funds over to them according to each man's abilities. To one he disbursed five thousand silver pieces, to a second two thousand, and to a third a thousand. Then

he went away. Immediately the man who received the five thousand went to invest it and made another five. In the same way the man who received the two thousand doubled his figure. The man who received the thousand went off instead and dug a hole in the ground, where he buried his master's money. After a long absence, the master of those servants came home and settled accounts with them. The man who had received five thousand came forward bringing the additional five. 'My lord,' he said, 'you let me have five thousand. See, I have made five thousand more.' His master said to him, 'Well done! You are an industrious and reliable servant. Since you were dependable in a small matter I will put you in charge of larger affairs. Come, share your master's joy!' The man who had received the two thousand then stepped forward. 'My lord,' he said, 'you entrusted me with two thousand and I have made two thousand more.' His master said to him, 'Cleverly done! You too are an industrious and reliable servant. Since you were dependable in a small matter I will put you in charge of larger affairs. Come, share your master's joy.'

"Finally the man who had received the thousand stepped forward. 'My lord,' he said, 'I knew you were a hard man. You reap where you did not sow and gather where you did not scatter, so out of fear I went off and buried your thousand silver pieces in the ground. Here is your money back.' His master exclaimed: 'You worthless, lazy lout! You know I reap where I did not sow and gather where I did not scatter. All the more reason to de-

> posit my money with the bankers, so that on my return I could have had it back with interest. You, there! Take the thousand away from him and give it to the man with the ten thousand. Those who have will get more until they grow rich, while those who have not will lose even the little they have. Throw this worthless servant into the darkness outside, where can wail and grind his teeth'" (Matthew 25:14–30).

The sums entrusted to each servant were not merely large. They were huge. Our version speaks of five, two, and a thousand silver pieces. Such amounts mean little to us, however. Matthew's text uses a word with even less meaning today, yet immediately intelligible to Jesus' hearers: *talanta*. Many versions translate this literally as "talents." This is not too helpful, either, since talents today designate natural aptitude or abilities. As we noted in chapter six above, a talent in Jesus' world was a sum of money, the largest there was, something like a million dollars today. Biblical commentators tell us that one talent was equivalent to the subsistence wage of an ordinary worker for fifteen years. Since the average life span in the ancient world was far shorter than it is today, it seems reasonable to calculate a man's working life (the years after childhood) at thirty years. According to this reckoning, therefore, the second servant received a sum equal to what a man might earn in an entire lifetime. The first servant received two-and-a-half times that amount. The sums involved were clearly enormous. Jesus' hearers recognized that at once, even if we do not.

This tells us something crucial about the story's central

character: the man going on a journey. He is not a bean counter. Generous in extending his trust, he is no less generous in reward. On his return from a long absence, he praises the first two servants for doubling the sums entrusted to them—something quite possible under the economic conditions of the day, though involving great risk. The words he speaks twice over, "You were dependable in a small matter," are deliberately ironic: The sum entrusted to each, and now doubled, was not small but huge. He backs up his praise by inviting each to "share your master's joy," words which clearly imply a handsome financial reward.

The people hearing the story now expect that the third servant will also receive generous treatment. By returning to his master the smaller but still enormous sum entrusted to him he has faithfully discharged his responsibility as custodian. True, he has not increased it, like the first two servants. But he has also avoided the risk of loss which they incurred by what today would rank as speculation.

How shocking, therefore, for Jesus' hearers to find the man not praised, but rebuked as a "worthless, lazy lout." In place of the reward that the first two servants received, this man, who has acted prudently according to the standards of the day, goes away empty-handed, banished into "outer darkness" to "wail and grind his teeth" in disappointed rage at his unjust treatment. The master, who up to this point in the story has seemed so generous, turns out to be no better than the greedy absentee landlords Jesus' hearers knew so well, squeezing the inhabitants of the land for every penny they could get out of them. The third servant's description of the master seems to be all too accurate: "I knew you were a hard man. You reap where you did not sow and gather where you did not scatter." With someone so grasping and unreasonable, prudence was the only safe policy. "Out of fear," the third servant explains, "I went off and buried your thousand silver pieces in the ground. Here is your money back."

How can we make sense of the story? Is the central figure, the master, simply arbitrary: generous with the first two servants, cruel to the third? So it would seem. The man's final action confirms this view. Taking the money that the third servant has faithfully preserved, he gives it to the first servant as an additional reward for the enormous risks he has taken in doubling the sum entrusted to him—an example of arbitrary injustice if there ever was one.

To make sense of the story we must ask not about the master's motives, but about those of the servants. The first two servants acted out of *trust.* A man who had entrusted them with so much, they reasoned, was clearly generous. He could be trusted. The third servant was motivated by *fear.* He says so himself: "Out of fear I went off and buried your thousand silver pieces in the ground." It is this fear that the parable condemns.

How often Jesus tells his followers, "Do not be afraid." He spoke these words to Peter after the miraculous catch of fish. When Peter protests, "Leave me, Lord. I am a sinful man," Jesus responds at once: "Do not be afraid. From now on you will be catching men" (Luke 5:8, 10). "Do not be afraid of anything," Jesus tells the Twelve in emphasizing God's providential care (Matthew 10:31). To the synagogue official, Jairus, pleading for the healing of his little daughter, Jesus says: "Fear is useless. What is needed in trust" (Mark 5:36). At the stilling of the storm on the lake he rebukes his disciples for their fear. "Why are you so terrified? Why are you lacking in faith?" (Mark 4:40; cf. 6:50 and John 6:20). When Jesus' three friends—Peter, James, and John—are "overcome with fear" at his transfiguration, Jesus tells them: "Get up! Do not be afraid" (Matthew 17:6f). He speaks the same words to Mary Magdalene and "the other Mary" on Easter morning (Matthew 28:10).

The master rebuked the third servant for lack of trust. The third servant did nothing bad. As we have seen, he fulfilled his responsibility. Like those at the king's left hand in the parable of the sheep and goats, which follows at once in Matthew's Gospel, the third servant is rejected not for anything he did, but for what he *failed* to do. Fear paralyzed him into inactivity.

The parable is about the one thing necessary: trust in the Lord who gives us his gifts not according to our deserving but according to his boundless generosity. The enormous sums entrusted to all three servants are like the gratuitous forgiveness of a huge debt extended in that other parable to the dishonest servant who pleaded for time to discharge a debt which, in reality, he had no hope of paying. At the end of that story the king's forgiveness of this unpayable debt, extended out of pity for the man's hopeless plight, is canceled because the man who has received the gift refuses to share it with a fellow servant who deserves forgiveness more than he does himself.

Concentrating on security above all, the third servant in this parable loses all. Burying the treasure entrusted to him seemed prudent. His understanding of prudence, however, was fatally flawed. The scripture scholar John L. McKenzie, who died in 1991, described this flaw when he said that for many Catholics

> prudence has long been, not the virtue by which one discerns the Christian thing to do, but the virtue by which one finds sound reason for evading the Christian thing to do. I have never read of any martyr who, if he or she had the course in Christian prudence which I had in the seminary, could not have evaded martyrdom with a good conscience.[1]

"The Christian thing to do" is to act boldly, like the first two servants in the story. For most of us that is difficult. Boldness is not our long suit. Like the third servant, we prefer to play it safe. The boldness of his two colleagues came not from themselves, but from their trust in the master's generosity. Burying our gift to keep it safe is like opting for a low-risk spiritual life, avoiding sin as far as possible but not loving much because of the risk involved: the risk of not loving wisely, the risk of having love betrayed, or not returned, and so being hurt.

Do you want to be certain that your heart will never be wounded as you journey through life? Then be sure to guard your heart carefully. Never give it away, and certainly never wear your heart on your sleeve. If you do that, however, your heart will shrink. The capacity to love is not diminished through use. It grows. What mother ever ran out of love because she had too many children? From the beginning of time loving mothers have found that with the birth of each child their ability to love is increased.

"Out of fear...I buried your thousand silver pieces," the third servant in the story tells his master. Jesus came *to cast out fear.*

> God did not send the Son into the world
> to condemn the world,
> but that the world might be saved through him.
> Whoever believes in him avoids condemnation,
> but whoever does not believe is already condemned
> for not believing in the name of God's only Son
> (John 3:17f).

To escape condemnation we don't need to establish a good-conduct record in some heavenly golden book: a series of stars after our name representing our prayers, sacrifices, and good works. Thinking we must do that is "not believing in the name of God's only Son." His name is synonymous with mercy, generosity, and love. Escaping condemnation, being saved, means one thing only: trusting him. It is as simple as that. We don't need to negotiate with God. We don't need to con him into being lenient. We couldn't do that even if we tried, for God is lenient already. He invites us to trust him. That is all.

Trusting him means risking all, our hearts first of all. It means loving: generously, recklessly, without limit and without conditions. Because that is the way God loves us. And doing that will mean suffering the wounds that love inevitably inflicts.

When the Spanish Carmelite Teresa of Ávila died at Alba de Tormes on October 4, 1582, the autopsy disclosed a scar on her heart. Years before, Teresa had described a vision of an angel piercing her heart with a fiery lance. The heart is preserved today, in a crystal reliquary, the wound clearly visible. Whatever the medical explanation of this phenomenon, the spiritual significance is clear. Teresa was a woman who loved deeply, passionately, even recklessly.

In so doing she received deep wounds, yet experienced joy deeper than all the wounds together. Here is what the English Carmelite, Ruth Burrows, writes about her:

> Teresa's will was identified with our Lord's. So everything she was, her many gifts and her weaknesses too, were brought into the orbit of her love and dedication. Union with Christ does not mean becoming someone different, renouncing our gifts, changing our temperament, but putting everything we have into our love for God and opening everything we have to his transforming influence....Teresa reached the full potential of personhood: what she was meant to be she became. This is holiness.[2]

With this parable of the three servants entrusted with enormous gifts on behalf of an absent master Jesus is inviting us to imitate the first two servants: to recognize the generosity of the one who gives us our gifts; and to trust him as we use and share his gifts to us, confident that when the Master returns we shall hear his voice, speaking to us personally, and with great tenderness: "Well done, good and faithful servant. Come share your master's joy!"

Question for Reflection

We pray in the first Eucharistic Prayer: "Though we are sinners, we trust in your mercy and love." Are God's mercy and love really the bottom line for me? Or is my trust elsewhere?

CHAPTER 11

"WILL THE SON OF MAN FIND FAITH?"

IN 1961 THE AUTHOR, JOSEPH HELLER, enriched the language with the title of a best-selling novel, later made into film, *Catch 22*. The phrase designates a hopeless situation. An example would be a worker applying for a job who is told he cannot be hired until he joins the union. When he applies for membership in the union, however, they tell him he cannot join until he has a job. Whichever way he turns he is stymied. One of Jesus' parables is about a person trapped in a Catch-22 situation.

> "Once there was a judge in a certain city who respected neither God nor man. A widow in that city kept coming to him saying, 'Give me my rights against my opponent.' For a time he refused, but finally he thought, 'I care little for God or man, but this widow is wearing me out. I am going to settle in her favor or she will end by doing me violence.'" The Lord said, "Listen to what the corrupt judge has to say. Will not God then do justice to his chosen who call out to him

> day and night? Will he delay long over them, do you suppose? I tell you, he will give them swift justice. But when the Son of Man comes, will he find any faith on the earth?" (Luke 18:2–8).

The statement in our version, that the judge "respected neither God nor man," is an abbreviation of Luke's text. This says that he "neither feared God nor regarded man." The judge's attitude crassly violated the injunction to judges by the good king Jehoshaphat:

> "Take care what you do, for you are judging, not on behalf of man, but on behalf of the LORD; he judges with you. And now let the fear of the LORD be upon you. Act carefully, for with the LORD, our God there is no injustice, no partiality, no bribe-taking" (2 Chronicles 19:6–7).

The judge in this story, without fear of God or regard for his reputation, is shameless. Appointed to uphold the law, he is himself an outlaw. Jesus' hearers would have nodded knowingly at the description. They knew such judges. The prohibition of injustice, partiality, and bribe-taking in the text just quoted confirms that these things were common. Rulers do not forbid nonexistent offenses. The prophet Amos confirms this with his castigation of judicial corruption in his day:

> Woe to those who turn judgment to wormwood
>   and cast justice to the ground!…
> Yes, I know how many are your crimes,
>   how grievous your sins:

> Oppressing the just, accepting bribes,
> repelling the needy at the gate! (Amos 5:7, 12).

We need not think of the widow in the story as old and infirm. Women married in their early teens in Jesus' day. This widow may well have been young. Her repeated appearance in court indicates that she was also vigorous. Young or old, however, widows in Jesus' day were among society's weakest members. It was a man's world. Women were not merely dependent on men. They were the property of men: of their fathers until marriage, and of their husbands thereafter. The last of the Ten Commandments lists "your neighbor's wife" among the property one must not covet (Exodus 20:17).

In a subsistence economy without any social safety net, a woman whose husband had died was vulnerable and destitute. The Jewish scriptures put widows and orphans under God's special protection:

> "You shall not wrong any widow or orphan. If you ever wrong them and they cry out to me, I will surely hear their cry. My wrath will flare up, and I will kill you with the sword; then your own wives will be widows, and your children orphans" (Exodus 22:21–23).

The prophets echo this message. Isaiah utters "woe" upon those who make "widows their plunder and orphans their prey" (10:1f). Zechariah says that God will "scatter with a whirlwind" those who "oppress the widow or the orphan, the alien or the poor" (7:10, 14). Though such texts were well known, Jesus' hearers understood that they would not influence a judge unmoved either by considerations of duty or by threats to his reputation.

The widow in Jesus' story is the victim of a corrupt system. An "opponent" is withholding her sole means of support—the remainder of her dowry or other inheritance. The Greek text, and the inferior position of women, suggests a male opponent: an in-law perhaps, a stepson by her husband's previous marriage, or possibly even her own son. If her rights are not vindicated, she will starve. Similar cases would have been familiar to Jesus' hearers. However regrettable, such instances of injustice had lost their power to shock. What would have shocked the hearers was the woman's brazen persistence.

Faithful to the age-old maxim that the squeaky wheel gets the most grease, she comes to court every day and makes a scene. This violated all societal norms. In her own quite different way the woman, too, is shameless.

At her first appearance the court officials doubtless explained to her that she could not be heard until she paid the usual fees. Since these went straight into the pockets of those demanding them, we would call them bribes. When the widow told them she was too poor to pay, they ignored her. Yet still she came. Those hearing the story recognize an impasse. Given the character of the judge, and the woman's poverty, they expect no resolution. Some problems, they realize, are insoluble.

Now comes a surprise. After days, perhaps many weeks, the widow suddenly achieves the breakthrough she has almost ceased hoping for. Without realizing it, she has found a chink in the seemingly impregnable armor of indifference with which the corrupt judge has covered himself. Consistent to the end, not out of any sense of justice but simply for his own convenience and to silence this public scold in his courtroom, he gives in, hears the woman's case, and quickly grants her what she has so long sought in vain.

Jesus' description of the judge's thought processes would have caused mirth in the hearers. "This widow is wearing me out," he reflects, and resolves to settle in her favor "or she will end by doing me violence." The humor is enhanced by language which, in Luke's original, is that of the boxing ring. The picture of one of society's weakest members pummeling with her fists a man of virtually unlimited power, with others at his beck and call, is laughable. To recapture the story's effect on its first hearers we might imagine a television skit in which an actor portraying the president of the United States ignores the verbal assaults of a homeless bag lady—until the woman hits him over the head with her bag, which turns out to be a water bomb that leaves the chief executive dripping wet.

The story's impact comes from its reversal of expectations at the end. A judge who neither fears God nor cares for what others think of him comes to fear a poor widow. A petitioner without power, both as a woman and because she has neither husband nor money, turns out to be anything but powerless. Her power lies in her persistence.

Like all Jesus' parables, this one describes conditions in God's kingdom: a state in which all normal worldly expectations are reversed. Where God reigns, Jesus is saying, victims claim their rights, often in surprising ways. And in God's kingdom victims obtain their rights. The weak and powerless are powerless no more. Wherever God reigns, Mary's words at the news that she was to the mother of God's Son are fulfilled: the proud are confused in their inmost thoughts; the might are toppled from their thrones; the lowly are raised to high places; the hungry are fed, and the rich are sent empty away (cf. Luke 1:51ff).

For the story's original hearers the use of a corrupt judge to illustrate God's goodness was so shocking as to require an explanation. Jesus supplies this with his two rhetorical questions:

> Will not God then do justice to his chosen who cry out to him day and night?
>
> Will he delay long over them, do you suppose?

At once Jesus answers these questions himself—and then puts a further question to the story's hearers, ourselves included:

> I tell you he will give them swift justice. But when the Son of Man comes, will he find any faith on the earth?

Most of Jesus' parables involve a similarity between the central figure and God. In this case the story turns on the *dissimilarity* between the corrupt judge and God. It is a "how much more" story. If even so depraved a judge as this one grants the petitioner her request in the end, *how much more* will God grant the prayers of those who ask him for their needs. God, Jesus is saying, is *not* like the corrupt judge. It is *not* difficult to get his attention. God is always more ready to hear than we to pray. God is *approachable.*

What is the point of praying, however, if God knows our needs before we do, and better than we do? Are prayers of petition or intercession attempts to change God's mind? If they were, God would be like the corrupt judge. And the point of the story, as we have seen, is that God is *not* like the corrupt judge. How does prayer work, then?

To that question there is no fully satisfying answer. Prayer, like everything to do with God, is a *mystery*: not in the sense that we can understand nothing about it, but that what we can understand is always less than the whole. One thing is certain. Prayer does not change God. Prayer changes *us*. It opens us up to the action of God in our lives, as the sun's rays open the flowers to their life-giving warmth and the nourishing moisture of dew and rain.

Prayer also reminds us of our *need* for God. How easily we forget that need, especially when the sun shines on us and things go well. Then we start to think we can make it on our own: by our cleverness, by luck, by pulling strings, by hard work, even by being so good that God will have to reward us.

We need to be reminded again and again that we can never make it on our own. No matter how clever we are; no matter how much luck we have; no matter how many strings we pull; no matter how hard we work or how hard we try to be good. Even when we have all these things going for us (and which of us has?), we *still need God.* God is the missing ingredient in life: the one without whom life is meaningless, without whose help all our striving, conniving, planning, struggling, and praying still fall pitifully short of the goal.

"Will not God do justice to his chosen who call out to him day and night?" Jesus asks at the story's conclusion. The answer would be obvious, even if Jesus did not supply it. *Of course* he will! First, however, God *wants* us to "cry out to him day and night." He wants us to pray and to keep on praying, even when it appears useless—because God seems to answer only with silence. Perseverance in prayer strengthens our desire and deepens our faith, very much as sustained physical exercise strengthens the muscles, heart, and lungs. Saint Augustine expresses this well:

> God wants our desire to be exercised in prayer, thus enabling us to grasp what he is preparing to give. ...We are small and limited vessels for the receiving of it....We shall have the greater capacity to receive [God's gifts], the more trustfully we believe, the more firmly we hope, the more ardently we desire.[1]

Saint Gregory the Great, Bishop of Rome from 590 to 604, says the same in a slightly different form:

> Holy desires grow with delay: if they fade through delay they are no desires at all.[2]

God always answers prayer, though not always at the time and in the manner that we want. In my eighth decade I am grateful to have lived long enough to be able to thank God for answering some of my prayers: "Not now," and others "Not ever." Nor will God keep us waiting until we bid high enough for the things we need. All that is certain. One thing alone is *uncertain*. Do we truly *believe* in a God who hears and answers our prayers? Do we really *trust* him? Or is our real trust elsewhere? In our own cleverness, in our good luck, in the strings we can pull, in our hard work, in the bribes we try to offer God in the form of prayers and sacrifices and good works?

None of those things is certain, Jesus tells us. There is certainty *only in God*. He alone can satisfy our deepest needs. Hence Jesus' final, insistent question:

When the Son of Man comes, will he find any faith on the earth?

Questions for Reflection

Do I persist in prayer, even when God seems to answer only with silence?

In asking God for my needs, and the needs of others, do I pray (in spirit if not literally): "Not what I want, Lord, but what you want"?

As I recall the things I have prayed for in the past, can I identify any requests which I am now thankful were never granted?

CHAPTER 12

BEGGARS AND BARGAINERS

THE REIGN OF GOD is like the case of the owner of an estate who went out at dawn to hire workmen for his vineyard. After reaching an agreement with them for the usual daily wage, he sent them out to his vineyard. He came out about midmorning and saw other men standing around the marketplace without work, so he said to them, "'You too go along to my vineyard and I will pay you whatever is fair.' At that they went away. He came out again around noon and midafternoon and did the same. Finally, going out in late afternoon he found still others standing around. To these he said, 'Why have you been standing here idle all day?' 'No one has hired us,' they told him. He said, 'You go to the vineyard too.' When evening came the owner of the vineyard said to his foreman, 'Call the workmen and give them their pay, but begin with the last group and end with the first.' When those hired late in the afternoon came up they received a full

> day's pay, and when the first group appeared they supposed they would get more; yet they received the same daily wage. Thereupon they complained to the owner, 'This last group did only an hour's work, but you have put them on the same basis as us who have worked a full day in the scorching heat.' 'My friend,' he said to one in reply, 'I do you no injustice. You agreed on the usual wage, did you not? Take your pay and go home. I intend to give this man who was hired last the same pay as you. I am free to do as I please with my money, am I not? Or are you envious because I am generous?'" (Matthew 20:1–15).

It seems terribly unfair, doesn't it? Even a child can see that it isn't right to pay people who have worked all day in the blazing sun no more than those who have worked only an hour. Many years ago I gave a conference on this parable to some fine sisters in St. Louis with whom I lived for seventeen years. When I had finished reading the story, I could see an elderly German sister in the front row frowning.

"They all get the same," she said. She was pretty burned up about it.

We *should* be burned up about it. If we're not, we haven't been listening; or the story is so familiar that it no longer disturbs us. This was not true of Jesus' hearers. To them the story was new. Living in a subsistence economy in which work was scarce, they would have found the story's opening appealing. People in need were being offered work at the prevailing daily wage. In the evening they would go home tired, but not empty-handed. Jesus' hearers would have been surprised, however, to find the hiring done by the vineyard owner himself, rather than by his foreman. What further surprises would the rabbi from Nazareth, already famous for his stories, have in store this time?

The first surprise was the order of payment at the end of the day. The hearers would have expected those hired first to be paid first. Even more surprising was the owner's unexpected generosity to those who had worked only an hour. The audience would have shared the expectation of those hired first that they would get more. When they did not, the hearers would have shared too the indignation of these full-time workers at the injustice of an employer who, up to now, had appeared not only just but generous.

To understand the story we have to realize that it is not about social justice. It is about God's generosity. Translated into the modern terms, and without replicating too literally conditions in today's labor market, the story might go somewhat as follows.

The central figure could be a rancher in one of the "salad factories" of California's San Fernando valley. Eager to harvest as much of his crop as possible before a threatened change in the weather, he goes to the hiring hall at dawn. The men he finds there are able-bodied and eager to work. They also know their rights. They *bargain* with the rancher about the conditions of work, and about their wages. When they strike a deal, they feel good about it. The work will be hard, but they know they will be well paid.

At intervals during the day, the foreman tells the rancher that more workers will be needed if they want to get in the whole harvest in time. The rancher makes repeated trips to town to hire additional help. Each time he encounters workers who are less promising. The men he finds lounging around in midafternoon are the dregs of the local labor market: drifters, panhandlers, winos. While those hired at dawn have been working in the hot sun, these men have spent another day idle, reflecting glumly on the hopelessness of their lot. There is no bargaining with men like that. As much out of pity as for any real help this sorry lot can offer, the rancher tells them, "Get into the truck, fellows. There's work for you out at my place."

At quitting time, those hired last are first in the pay line. These are the men whom life has passed over. They have learned through bitter experience that every man's hand is against them. They wish now that something had been said about wages before they got into the rancher's truck a couple of hours earlier.

The first man in line receives his pay envelope. He rips it open—and can't believe his eyes. It contains a whole day's pay! He stands there dazed, tears of joy welling up in his eyes. He expected to be swindled. Instead, he has been treated generously—far more generously, he knows, than he deserves.

Meanwhile, news of what the first men in line are receiving is being passed back to those in the rear. These are the men who have worked hard all day. They calculate how much *they* will receive at the same hourly rate. Imagine their indignation when they receive exactly what they had bargained for in the early morning. They protest angrily to the rancher.

"It's my money, isn't it?" he answers them. "If I want to be generous to someone else, what's that to you?"

We are left with the injustice. The story begins to make sense only when we ask: Who was happy? Who was disappointed? And why? Those who were happy were the men hired last and paid first. They had not bargained. They had nothing to bargain with. They were little better than beggars. It was these beggars, however, who went away happy, while the bargainers were unhappy.

Why? Not because they had struck a bad bargain. No, at the beginning of the day they knew it was a *good* bargain. Nor were they unhappy because the bargain was not kept. On the contrary, it was kept to the letter. At the end of the day, however, they thought of something that had never occurred to them when they were hired. They thought they deserved more.

The men who went away happy did not appeal to what they deserved. They knew they deserved very little. The only thing they could appeal to was the rancher's generosity. *That* is the key to a right relationship with God, Jesus says. Appeal to God's generosity and you will be flooded with joy. Appeal to what you *deserve*, and God will give it to you. God is always just. He never short-changes us. When we discover, however, how little we actually deserve, we'll probably be disappointed.

We know the story as the parable of the laborers in the vineyard. A better title would be the parable of the beggars and the bargainers. The story is important for us. It flies in the face of everything we've been taught. Society says we should *not* be beggars. We should *work* for what we get, not depend on handouts. In everyday life that is fine. With God, however, different standards apply. He loves to give handouts! To receive them, however, we need to stand before him empty-handed, appealing (if we must appeal at all) not to God's justice but to his mercy. More, we must forget about keeping track of what we think we "deserve" and stop worrying that others whom we consider "less deserving" (or not deserving at all!) share the Lord's overflowing bounty with us.

The full-time workers in this story resemble the elder son in the story of the merciful father, angry at the undeserved welcome extended to his shiftless younger brother. Like those who had worked all day in the vineyard, the elder brother thought he had been short-changed. He was mistaken. "Everything I have is yours," his father told him (Luke 15:31). What more could he have received than that? The elder brother in that story needed to stop keeping score and join in welcoming the family member who, despite his folly and sin, was still his brother.

Robert Capon's interpretations of the parables sometimes go "over the top." In this instance, however, he is right on:

> Bookkeeping is the only punishable offense in the kingdom of heaven. For in that happy state, the *books* are ignored forever, and there is only the *Book* of life....If the world could have been saved by bookkeeping it would have been saved by Moses, not Jesus. The law was just fine. And God gave it a good thousand years or so to see if anyone could pass a test like that. But when nobody did—when it became perfectly clear that there was "no one who was righteous, not even one" (Romans 3:10; Psalm 14:1–3), that "both Jews and Gentiles alike were all under the power of sin" (Romans 3:9)—God gave up on salvation by the books. He canceled everybody's records in the death of Jesus and rewarded us all, equally and fully, with a new creation in the resurrection of the dead.[1]

Are you a bargainer with God—or a beggar? If you want to experience God's *justice*, be a bargainer. If you'd rather experience his *generosity*, however, be a beggar. Then you will know the joy of Mary at the news that she was to be the mother of God's Son: "The hungry he has given every good thing, / while the rich he has sent empty away" (Luke 1:53).

Ask the Lord who bestows his gifts not according to our deserving but according to his boundless generosity to give you that hunger which longs to be fed; that emptiness which yearns to be filled. Stand beneath his cross and say, in the words of the old evangelical hymn: *Nothing in my hand I bring, simply to your cross I cling.*

Questions for Reflection

Do I wonder sometimes whether it is really worthwhile to keep on trying to be faithful to God and all his claims on me?

Does it bother me when I see other people who have more than I do, especially when they seem undeserving?

Do I take time each day to count the blessings I *do* have, and to thank God for them?

CHAPTER 13

THE MAN GOD HELPED

JESUS' PARABLES ARE WORKS OF FICTION. That is, they are made up stories. Like many fictional works, they may reflect actual incidents or experiences. The story of the woman searching for her lost coin, and when she found it throwing a party that possibly cost more than the coin she had just recovered, may have originated in an incident from Jesus' youth. The story of the Good Samaritan may have been inspired by an actual mugging on the dangerous road between Jerusalem and Jericho. The truth of the stories does not depend, however, on their having actually happened. Jesus' parables are good examples of how fictional, made-up stories can convey profound truth.

An indication that Jesus' parables are fiction is the fact that only one of the characters in them has a name: Lazarus, the poor beggar at the rich man's gate whose fate in this life is dramatically reversed after death:

> "Once there was a rich man who dressed in purple and linen and feasted splendidly every day. At his

gate lay a beggar named Lazarus who was covered with sores. Lazarus longed to eat the scraps that fell from the rich man's table. The dogs even came and licked his sores. Eventually, the beggar died. He was carried by angels to the bosom of Abraham. The rich man likewise died and was buried. From the abode of the dead where he was in torment, he raised his eyes and saw Abraham afar off, and Lazarus resting in his bosom.

"He called out, 'Father Abraham, have pity on me. Send Lazarus to dip the tip of his finger in water to refresh my tongue, for I am tortured in these flames.' 'My child,' replied Abraham, 'remember that you were well off in your lifetime, while Lazarus was in misery. Now he has found consolation here, but you have found torment. And that is not all. Between you and us there is fixed a great abyss, so that those who might wish to cross from here to you cannot do so, nor can anyone cross from your side to us.'

"'Father, I ask you, then,' the rich man said, 'send him to my father's house where I have five brothers. Let him be a warning to them so that they may not end in this place of torment.' Abraham answered. 'They have Moses and the prophets. Let them hear them.' 'No, Father Abraham,' replied the rich man. 'But if someone would only go to them from the dead, then they would repent.' Abraham said to him, 'If they do not listen to Moses and the prophets, they will not be convinced even if one should rise from the dead'" (Luke 16:19–31).

Like many of the parables, this one is a story of contrasts. These are stark, both in this life and in the hereafter. The rich man has every comfort that money can buy. The beggar at his gate has only his name: Lazarus, a word that means "may God help" or "the one whom God helps." This name is significant, as we shall see.

The rich man's clothing ("purple and linen") and lifestyle (he "feasted splendidly every day") proclaim abundance and luxury. He is far above the social-economic level of Jesus' ordinary hearers. According to the conventional morality of the day, however, which viewed wealth as a sign of God's blessing, the hearers would have admired the rich man as an upright pillar of society. Moreover, it is unlikely that they sympathized with Lazarus. They saw beggars like him every day. Such people, they assumed, were receiving their just deserts from God. This was the assumption of Job's "comforters." Much of that book is taken up with the attempts of Job's friends to convince him that his sufferings are deserved, an idea that Job heatedly rejects.

The idea that worldly suffering must be a punishment for sin was also implicit in the question Jesus' disciples put to him about the man born blind: "Rabbi, was it his sin or that of his parents that caused him to be born blind?" To which Jesus answers: "Neither. It was no sin, either of this man or of his parents"(John 9:2–3). The parable of the Rich Man and Lazarus, like the book of Job, also repudiates the idea that suffering is always the result of personal sin.

The description of Lazarus' plight is remarkably similar to that of the younger son in the far country in the parable of the merciful father and the two lost sons. The young man in that story "longed to fill his belly with the husks that were fodder for the pigs" (Luke 15:16). Lazarus "longed to eat the scraps that fell from the rich man's table." To understand this description we need to know the eating customs of the day. Food was eaten with the fingers, which were wiped afterward with pieces of flat bread that were then cast aside to be eaten by the household dogs. The persistent Gentile woman, beseeching Jesus to heal her little daughter, reminded him of this custom when she said: "Even the dogs under the table eat the family's leavings" (Mark 7:28).

The animals that lick Lazarus' open sores are not pets, however, but stray dogs such as one still sees in Third World countries, cared for and fed by no one and feeding on offal and garbage. Such dogs were a plague in the ancient world. They licked up the blood of Naboth, murdered by the wicked king Ahab because Naboth refused to exchange his ancestral property next to the king's palace for land that Ahab offered him elsewhere. God sent the prophet Elijah to warn Ahab that his crime would not go unpunished: "In the place where the dogs licked up the blood of Naboth, the dogs shall lick up your blood, too" (1 Kings 21:19).

The contrast between the two men in the story extends to the smallest details. The rich man is "clothed in purple and fine linen." Lazarus is "covered with sores"—and apparently little else, since nothing else is mentioned and dogs lick his sores. The rich man "feasted splendidly every day." Lazarus "longed to eat the scraps" of bread discarded by the rich man and his guests at their daily banquets. The rich man is active. Lazarus is passive, unable even to fend off the animals whose attentions increase his misery. We are not even told that Lazarus begged. He simply lies there at the rich man's gate, unnoticed by the rich man as he passes in and out each day. The rich man is an insider, Lazarus the quintessential outsider.

Death reverses these contrasts. "The beggar died," Jesus tells us with stark economy of language. The description becomes richer, however, as we hear about Lazarus (still passive) being lifted out of this world, in which he had been a neglected outsider, and "carried by angels to the bosom of Abraham." Lazarus is now the quintessential insider.

Unlike Lazarus, the rich man has a funeral: "The rich man likewise died and was buried." Now *he* becomes the outsider, buried in the ground of this world. Where previously he had "feasted splendidly," now he is "in torment." His daily feasting is replaced by craving for a drop of water to cool his tongue, parched from the flames that surround him.

And now the rich man does something he has not done before. For the first time, Jesus tells us, "he raised his eyes and saw Lazarus"—no longer near, however, but "afar off" in Abraham's bosom, in the place of honor like the "disciple whom Jesus loved" leaning on the Lord's breast at the Last Supper (cf. John 13:23ff). Why is Lazarus in *Abraham's* bosom? Because the patriarch was a model of the hospitality expected of the wealthy in the ancient world, a duty the rich man had signally failed to provide for the poor beggar whom he passed daily at his gate, yet never saw. Hearing Abraham's name, Jesus' hearers would have recalled at once the well-known story of the patriarch extending hospitality to three strangers who turn out to be messengers from God, angels sent to tell Abraham that his aged wife, Sarah, hitherto childless, will bear a son in whom "all the nations of the earth are to find blessing" (Genesis 18:18).

The significance of Lazarus' name is now manifest. He

is the man whom God helps. Ignored in life—by the rich man, his guests, and everyone else—Lazarus is disclosed at death to be especially dear to God, who sends angels to carry him to a place of consolation and honor. This would have puzzled the story's first hearers, accustomed to thinking that unfortunates like Lazarus were receiving the just reward for their sins.

Equally disturbing for the hearers would have been the rich man's punishment. This cannot have been the consequence of his wealth, for Abraham was rich. The punishment would have seemed especially unjust since the rich man had received no warning of the importance of passing through his gate to aid Lazarus, and no opportunity to repent and atone for his sin. Like those on the king's left hand in Matthew's parable of the sheep and the goats, the rich man is punished not for anything he did, but for what he failed to do.[1] He failed to heed the command of the Jewish scriptures to "love your neighbor as yourself" (Leviticus 19:18), called by Jesus one of the two basic laws of God's kingdom (cf. Mark 12:31).

In that other parable of judgment those at the king's left protest at the injustice of their condemnation, demanding to know when they have ever transgressed God's law. The rich man in this parable utters no protest. Seeming to recognize the justice of his fate, he merely asks that Lazarus (still passive) be sent "to dip the tip of his finger in water and refresh my tongue, for I am tortured in these flames." The rich man has forgotten nothing and learned nothing. He still assumes that he is in charge and can command others to do his bidding. Significantly, however, he directs his request not to Lazarus but to Abraham, a wealthy man like himself, but, unlike him, a model of hospitality.

Abraham's response is gentle. Addressing his petitioner as "my child," Abraham discloses that the separation between the rich man and Lazarus, formerly the result merely of the former's neglect and hence reversible, is now permanent because established by God. Abraham's use of the passive, "between you and us there is fixed a great abyss," is a way of saying: "God has fixed an abyss between us." The biblical writers often use the passive in this way, as a circumlocution to describe the works of the all-holy God whose Hebrew name, Jahweh, was so sacred that, when read aloud, it was always replaced by the word Adonai, "Lord."

The dialogue which follows takes the parable to a new level. Up to now it can be read as an illustration of Jesus' contrast between rich and poor in the Sermon on the Plain: "Blest are you poor...Woe to you rich" (Luke 6:20, 24). The rich man, who for the first time has "raised his eyes" and seen Lazarus, now makes his first move to repair his previous failure by helping those in need. Never having encountered refusal in life, and still assuming that others are there to serve him, he asks Abraham to send Lazarus to his brothers on earth as "a warning, so they may not end in this place of torment." Abraham's response to this seemingly reasonable request sounds callous: "They have Moses and the prophets. Let them hear them." The rich man immediately counters with an objection as plausible as his original request. "No, Father Abraham....But if someone would only go to them from the dead, then they would repent."

Across the distance of almost six decades I can still recall my reaction to the annual reading of this gospel in my youth.[2] "He's got a point there," I thought each time I heard the rich man's objection. "If someone were to go to them from the dead, that would shake them up!" Enlightenment came one Sunday during my teens, when, listening to this gospel, I realized: *Hey. A man did rise from the dead once. It didn't shake anyone up. The only people who believed in him were those who had believed in him before, and even they had to overcome initial skepticism.*

Luke's language confirms this youthful insight. The rich man speaks of a *return:* "if someone would only go to them from the dead." Abraham, on the other hand, speaks not of return but of *resurrection*: "If they do not listen to Moses and the prophets, they will not be convinced even if one should rise from the dead." "Moses and the prophets" means simply "holy scripture"—for Jesus and his hearers the Torah. Jesus uses Abraham's words of refusal to the rich man's final request to state what Jesus himself has already experienced many times over: signs and wonders, no matter how dramatic, are never sufficient to compel faith in those who have not already gained faith through attentive reading or hearing of God's word. The greatest of all Jesus' signs was the empty tomb of Easter morning. It was the occasion of faith to one man only: the disciple whom Jesus loved, as he is called in John's gospel (cf. John 20:2–8). Jesus' other followers came to faith in the resurrection only through seeing the risen Lord. Those who had refused to believe in him before the crucifixion had a simple explanation for the empty tomb: Jesus' disciples stole his body while the soldiers guarding the tomb slept (cf. Matthew 28:12–15).

Abraham's seemingly callous reminder that the rich man's brothers need only "Moses and the prophets" to avoid his fate is Jesus' way of telling his hearers, ourselves included, that present circumstances are always enough for us to believe in God and serve him. Most of us, most of the time, live and work in circumstances that are far from ideal. Confronted with our modest achievements, we plead that they are a consequence of our limited opportunities. When things change and we get into *better* circumstances, we shall be able to accomplish so much more.

That is an illusion. The golden opportunities that beckon on the other side of the horizon will never arrive if we are not using the opportunities, however inadequate, that are before us right now. It is here and now, in the present moment (the only time we ever have) that we are called to faith in God, and to generous service of God and others—and not somewhere else, tomorrow, when everything changes at the touch of some magic wand and our lives cease to be drab and become wonderful.

How drab, boring, and dull life in the carpenter's shop at Nazareth must have been. How cramped and narrow Jesus' existence must have been during those long "hidden years" in that backward little village before his brief public ministry. Yet Jesus *chose* that limited, inadequate situation rather than a brilliant career at the center of the sophisticated world. Why?

He did so to show us that God, who (as Scripture repeatedly testifies) is especially close to the poor, is most often encountered in poor circumstances, in the humble and humdrum events of every day. We do not need to make a long journey, to go on pilgrimage, to find God. He is always close to us, even when we stray far from him. That is absolutely certain. That is the good news. One thing alone is *uncertain*. Do *we* really want to be close to *him*?

If so, we need to heed the seemingly banal yet sure counsel of Abraham. We must listen to God's word. If we do this, not just occasionally, but faithfully—day after day, week by week, and year after year—we shall find ourselves strengthened, guided, and fed. Faithful, patient sitting at the Lord's feet, listening and pondering his words like Mary of Bethany[3] will enable us to understand the words of Cleopas and his unnamed companion[4] after their encounter with the risen Lord at Emmaus on the first Easter evening: "Were not our hearts burning inside us as he talked to us on the road and explained the Scriptures to us?" (Luke 24:32).

If we wish to be close to the Lord, we need to do also what the rich man in the parable *failed* to do. We need to *see* the needs of those around us. And like the despised outsider in the parable of the Good Samaritan, we need to minister to those needs in caring, costing ways. The Lord seldom demands heroism. Often a kind word, a friendly gesture, or an encouraging smile is enough. But unless we are open to the needs of those we encounter on life's way, and are trying to meet those needs, we shall discover one day that we have lived far from God, no matter how many prayers we have said. And if we have lived far from God in this life, we shall live far from him in eternity. God's judgment is not something imposed on us from outside. It is his ratification of the judgment we make in this life by the way we choose to live.

Clearly this is a parable of judgment. God's judgment need not be fearful, however. In reality it is part of the good news. The judgment meted out in this parable to Lazarus—passive throughout and speaking never a word—assures us that the inarticulate, the weak, the poor, the marginalized and neglected, are especially dear to God. Lazarus, the man whom God helped, tells us that in the kingdom Jesus came to proclaim the blind see, the deaf hear, the lame walk and run without growing weary; those who hope in the Lord renew their strength and soar as on eagles' wings; the tone-deaf sing like Kiri Te Kanawa and Placido Domingo; the poor are made rich; the hungry feast at the banquet of eternal life; the sorrowful are filled with laughter and joy; and those who are ostracized and persecuted because of the Son of Man receive their unbelievably great reward.

That, too, is the gospel proclaimed by this parable. That is the good news.

Questions for Reflection

Do I live too much in the future, feeding on illusions of a wonderful tomorrow while neglecting the opportunities before me today?

Are there opportunities for service I am neglecting, people I see every day whom I could help yet never do?

CHAPTER 14

"Go Home"

THEY CAME TO GERASENE territory on the other side of the lake. As [Jesus] got out of the boat, he was immediately met by a man from the tombs who had an unclean spirit. The man had taken refuge among the tombs; he could no longer be restrained, even with a chain. In fact, he had frequently been secured with handcuffs and chains but had pulled the chains apart and smashed the fetters. No one had proved strong enough to tame him. Uninterruptedly night and day, amid the tombs and on the hillsides, he screamed and gashed himself with stones. Catching sight of Jesus at a distance, he ran up and did him homage, shrieking in a loud voice, "Why meddle with me, Jesus, Son of God Most High? I implore you in God's name, do not torture me!" (Jesus had been saying to him, "Unclean spirit, come out of the man!") "What is your name?" Jesus asked him. "Legion is my name," he answered. "There are hundreds of us." He pleaded hard with

> Jesus not to drive them away from that neighborhood.
>
> It happened that a large herd of swine was feeding there on the slope of the mountain. "Send us into the swine," they begged him. "Let us enter them." He gave the word, and with it the unclean spirits came out and entered the swine. The herd of about two thousand went rushing down the bluff into the lake, where they began to drown. The swineherds ran off and brought the news to field and village, and the people came to see what had happened. As they approached Jesus, they caught sight of the man who had been possessed by Legion sitting fully clothed and perfectly sane, and they were seized with fear. The spectators explained what had happened to the possessed man, and told them about the swine. Before long they were begging him to go away from their district. As Jesus was getting into the boat, the man who had been possessed was pressing to accompany him. Jesus did not grant his request, but told him instead: "Go home to your family and make it clear to them how much the Lord in his mercy has done for you." At that the man went off and began to proclaim throughout the Ten Cities what Jesus had done for him. They were all amazed at what they heard (Mark 5:1–20).

Of all the miracles of healing in the gospels, this is the most bizarre. It takes place in Gentile territory. That is evident from the presence of the large herd of pigs—unclean animals whose flesh could not be eaten by Jews. The man whom Jesus heals is mentally ill. According to the ideas of the day, he is possessed by demons. As in his other healings, Jesus acts within the framework of these ideas, the only ones available in that prescientific age. Exactly what happened—in particular the meaning of the dialogue between the demons and Jesus—we can no longer say. We must leave that to the Scripture scholars. Even without their help, however, it is not difficult to understand why the people of the region begged Jesus to depart. The loss of such a large herd of pigs was a major disaster for the local economy. The wonder is not that they asked him to leave, but that they did not compel him to do so by force.

The important element of the story for us is the man's experience *after* his healing. Jesus has restored him to a normal life from an existence that was little better than a living death. No wonder that the man "was pressing to accompany" Jesus. Any of us would have done the same. And how crushed the man must have been at Jesus' response. Jesus did not grant his request, but told him instead, "Go home to your family and make it clear to them how much the Lord in his mercy has done for you." "To my *family*?" we can hear the man saying. They were the people who had driven him out of his mind in the first place. At home everyone would point him out, whisper about him, laugh at him. What would happen to his newfound sanity then?

With a cold, dead weight on his heart, the man watches Jesus and his friends prepare to leave. He stands on the lakeshore as they make the boat ready. Jesus sits in the bow while the disciples wade out on each side of the boat, pushing it until it floats. They scramble over the sides, row away from shore, and set up mast and sail. The wind fills it, and the boat gathers sway. Still standing on the beach, the man Jesus has healed sees the boat getting smaller and smaller until it is just a blip on the distant horizon. He thinks: Out there is the man who changed my life, the kindest, the most understanding, the most wonderful man I ever met. It must have been a long time before he found courage to turn round and climb the cliff again, obeying Jesus' command, "Go home to your family and make it clear to them how much the Lord in his mercy has done for you."

The Lord is saying the same to you right now. By pondering his wonderful stories you have been with him, and he with you, in a special way. Perhaps you have experienced the Lord's touch, the uplifting presence of his Holy Spirit. Maybe, like Cleopas and his unnamed companion on the road to Emmaus on that first Easter afternoon, there were times when you felt your heart burning within you. You would like to prolong the experience. That is natural. But it cannot be. And it would not be good for you even if it were possible.

When Jesus reached Emmaus, Luke tells us, "he acted as if he were going farther. But they pressed him: 'Stay with us. It is nearly evening—the day is practically over.'" Jesus granted this request, but only long enough to make himself known to them in the breaking of the bread. "Whereupon," Luke writes, "he vanished from their sight." The encounter left his two friends changed. Forgetting the late hour and their weariness, "they got up immediately and returned to Jerusalem, where they found the Eleven and the rest of the company assembled. They were greeted with, 'The Lord has been raised! It is true! He has appeared to Simon.' Then they recounted what had happened on the road and how they had come to know him in the breaking of the bread" (Luke 24:33–35).

Mary Magdalene's experience with the risen Lord was

similar. She, too, failed to recognize Jesus at first, like most of those to whom he appeared after his Resurrection. Why? Because Jesus was changed. He had not returned to earthly life. That ended on Calvary. At the Resurrection Jesus was raised to a new life, beyond death and this world. That explains why Peter and "the disciple whom Jesus loved" found the Lord's burial wrappings in the empty tomb.[1] He left them behind because he would never need them again.

When Jesus raised Lazarus from death, by contrast, his friend emerged from the tomb "bound hand and foot with linen strips, his face wrapped in a cloth."[2]

Lazarus *had* returned to life. He would need his burial wrappings again, when he died a second time.

Because Jesus had been raised to new life beyond death, most of those who saw him after the Resurrection did not recognize him at first, rather as we fail to recognize a friend we have not seen for decades. Only after observing the person's expressions and gestures do we realize that it is, indeed, the person we once knew, changed, to be sure, yet undoubtedly the same. Those who saw the risen Lord seem to have had a similar experience.

Mary Magdalene recognized the risen Lord only when he spoke her name. She must have reached out to embrace him, for Jesus said at once, "Do not cling to me." Her desire to resume the previous relationship of intimacy with the Lord was understandable. Yet Jesus refused her, as he refused the madman he healed at Gerasa. In doing so he made Mary Magdalene, as he had made the madman, his messenger and witness: "Go to my brothers and tell them, 'I am ascending to my Father and your Father to my God and your God!'" Mary Magdalene went to the disciples. "I have seen the Lord!" she announced (John 20:17–18).

Whenever the Lord comes to us, he does so not so that we can luxuriate in the warmth of a beautiful spiritual experience. The experience is given to us, like all God's gifts, not for ourselves, but for others. The risen Lord comes to us, as he came to Mary Magdalene, to send us to our sisters and brothers, to empower us to proclaim, by the inner quality of our lives if not by our words, "I have seen the Lord."

Jesus' followers fulfilled that sending in the first generation after the Resurrection. They did it, as Christians have done so often in history, without even realizing what they were doing. Luke tells about it in the Acts of the Apostles. Indignant that Peter and John had caused a public sensation by healing a lame beggar and were "proclaiming the resurrection of the dead in the person of Jesus," the Jewish authorities had the two confined in jail overnight. In the morning they demanded to know:

> "By what power or in whose name have men of your stripe done this?" Then Peter, filled with the Holy Spirit, spoke up: "Leaders of the people! Elders! If we must answer today for a good deed done to a cripple and explain how he was restored to health, then you and all the people of Israel must realize that it was done in the name of Jesus Christ the Nazorean whom you crucified and whom God raised from the dead. In the power of that name this man stands before you perfectly sound. This Jesus is 'the stone rejected by you the builders which has become the cornerstone.' There is no salvation in anyone else, for there is no other name in the whole world given to men by which we are to be saved.

> "Observing the self-assurance of Peter and John, and realizing that the speakers were uneducated men of no standing, the questioners were amazed. Then they recognized these men as having been with Jesus" (Acts 4:7–13).

Do people recognize the same of us—that we also have been with Jesus?

We began with the story of Jesus healing a man of mental illness. We close with another story. Like the parables, it is fiction. And like them, it contains an important spiritual truth:

When the Lord Jesus returned to heaven at the Ascension, the angels wanted to know everything he had done on earth. So Jesus told them how he had gone about doing good, healing the sick, and teaching people about the freely given love of God.

"That's wonderful, Lord," the angels said. "But now that you're no longer on earth, won't people soon forget about what you have done and said?"

"Oh no," Jesus explained. "I founded a church. I chose twelve men to be its first bishops. I spent three years teaching them: how to pray, how to heal people, how to free them from their burdens, how to teach others about God's freely given love. They are going to carry on my work."

"That's all well and good, Lord," the angels replied. "But we know how fickle and unreliable these human beings are. How do you know that they will keep on doing all those things you trained them to do? How do you know that they will remain faithful?"

At that the Lord fell silent. He looked down and seemed to be thinking. Then he looked up and, with that beautiful, radiant smile of his, said very simply, "I *trust* them."

Select Bibliography

The literature on the parables is vast. These books have helped me:

Raymond E. Brown *et al.* (editors), *The Jerome Biblical Commentary*. Englewood Cliffs, N.J.: Prentice Hall, 1968.

_____, *The New Jerome Biblical Commentary*, Englewood Cliffs, N.J.: Prentice Hall, 1990.

Robert Farrar Capon, *The Parables of Grace*. Grand Rapids, Mich.: Eerdmans, 1991.

_____, *The Parables of Judgement*, Grand Rapids, MI: Eerdmans, 1993.

John R. Donahue, *The Gospel in Parable*. Minneapolis: Augsburg Fortress, 1988.

Ruth Etchells, *A Reading of the Parables of Jesus*. London: Darton, Longman & Todd, 1998.

David M. Granskou, *Preaching on the Parables*. Philadelphia: Fortress, 1972.

Joachim Jeremias, *The Parables of Jesus*. New York: Scribner, 1972.

Heinrich Kahlefeld, *Gleichnisse und Lehrstücke*. Frankfurt: Knecht, 1963.

Otto Knoch, *Wer Ohren hat, der höre. Die Botschaft der Gleichnisse Jesu*. Stuttgart: Katholisches Bibelwerk, 1983.

B.W. Maturin, *Practical Studies on the Parables of Our Lord*. London: Longmans Green, 1920.

Bernard Brandon Scott, *Hear Then the Parable*. Minneapolis: Augsburg Fortress, 1989.

Notes

INTRODUCTION

1. St. Ephraem, *On the Diatessaron* 1:18; *Office of Readings*, Sunday, Week 6.

CHAPTER 1

1. *An Essay on the Development of Christian Doctrine* (London, 1845), 39.
2. 11:27, *Revised Standard Version*; a more vivid rendering than the NAB: "he persevered as if he were looking for the invisible God."
3. "Jesus used realistic images from daily life that caught his hearers' attention by their vividness and narrative color. Yet his parables have a surprising twist: the realism is shattered and the hearers know that something more is at stake than a homey illustration to drive home a point. The parables raise questions, unsettle the complacent, and challenge the hearers to reflection and inquiry." *The New Jerome Biblical Commentary* (Englewood Cliffs, N.J.: Prentice Hall, 1990), p.1366 No. 72.
4. "The parables were modified in the teaching of the community;...most allegorical features are almost universally regarded by modern scholars as expansions made by the primitive Church." John L. McKenzie, in: *The Jerome Biblical Commentary* (Englewood Cliffs, N.J.: Prentice Hall, 1968), No. 43:88.
5. No. 42:25.

CHAPTER 2

1. The question "would shock those to whom the parable is directed and amuse the audience." John R. Donahue, *The Gospel in Parable* (Philadelphia: Fortress, 1988), p. 148.
2. Donahue, *op. cit.,* p. 149.

CHAPTER 4

1. *The New Jerome Biblical Commentary* p. 1243, No. 75:148.
2. When Moses asked to see God's glory, God replied: "My face you cannot see, for no man sees me and still lives....I will set you in the hollow the rock and will cover you with my hand until I have passed by" (Exodus 33:18–22).

CHAPTER 5

1. Cited from Peter Hebblethwaite, *Pope John XXIII: Shepherd of the Modern World* (New York: Doubleday, 1984), p. 303.

CHAPTER 9

1. Cf. Thomas Merton (ed.), *The Prison Meditations of Father Alfred Delp* (Herder & Herder: New York, 1963), p. 3.
2. *Orthodoxy* (New York: Dodd, Mead, 1954), pp. 289f.

CHAPTER 10

1. Cited from Emmanuel James McCarthy, "In appreciation of a Catholic scholar" in: *America*, May 18, 1991, 534f at 535.
2. Ruth Burrows, "The way to perfection" in: *The Tablet,* Oct. 16, 1982, 1032f, at 1032.

CHAPTER 11

1. Letter to Proba, 130; Office of Readings for the 29th Sunday in Ordinary Time.
2. Homily 25 on the Gospels; Office of Readings for St. Mary Magdalene.

CHAPTER 12

1. Robert Farrar Capon, *The Parables of Judgment* (Grand Rapids, Mich.: Eerdmans, 1991), 55f.

CHAPTER 13

1. Cf. Matthew 25:41–45.
2. As an Anglican, I heard it on the First Sunday after Trinity. In the Roman Missal it was assigned to Thursday after the Second Sunday in Lent.
3. Cf. Luke 10:38–42.
4. Whom some commentators think may have been Cleopas' wife.

CHAPTER 14

1. Cf. John 20:3–7
2. John 11:44

About the Author

A native of New York City, where he was born in 1928 as the son and grandson of priests in the Episcopal Church, John Jay Hughes served as an Anglican priest for six years before entering the Catholic Church in 1960. In 1968 he was conditionally ordained deacon and priest by the late Bishop Joseph Höffner of Münster. He has taught at the Catholic University of Leuven in Belgium and at the Divinity School of St. Louis University, served as pastor of three parishes, and in diocesan administration. A priest of the archdiocese of St. Louis, he is the author of nine previous books and several hundred articles and book reviews.